总主编 梁为祥

（第2版）

A Coursebook on English-Chinese Translation
(Second Edition)

英译汉教程

主　编　王金铨　徐　黎
副主编　何山华　刘　猛　王鉴莺　李　涛
　　　　宋　煜　佘月月　宋学东

西安交通大学出版社
XI'AN JIAOTONG UNIVERSITY PRESS
国家一级出版社
全国百佳图书出版单位

图书在版编目(CIP)数据

英译汉教程/王金铨,徐黎主编.—2版.—西安:西安交通大学出版社,2021.9
ISBN 978-7-5693-2287-3

Ⅰ.①英… Ⅱ.①王… ②徐… Ⅲ.①英语－翻译－高等学校－教材 Ⅳ.①H315.9

中国版本图书馆 CIP 数据核字(2021)第 192871 号

英译汉教程(第2版)
YING YI HAN JIAOCHENG
主　　编　王金铨　徐　黎
责任编辑　蔡乐芊
责任校对　焦　铭

出版发行	西安交通大学出版社 (西安市兴庆南路1号　邮政编码 710048)
网　　址	http://www.xjtupress.com
电　　话	(029)82668357　82667874(市场营销中心) (029)82668315(总编办)
传　　真	(029)82668280
印　　刷	陕西金德佳印务有限公司
开　　本	720mm×1000mm　1/16　印张　14　字数　266千字
版次印次	2021年9月第1版　2021年9月第1次印刷
书　　号	ISBN 978-7-5693-2287-3
定　　价	54.90元

如发现印装质量问题,请与本社市场营销中心联系、调换。
订购热线:(029)82665248　(029)82665249
投稿热线:(029)82665371
读者信箱:xjtu_rw@163.com

版权所有　侵权必究

Preface
（前言）

翻译课是普通高等院校英语专业的一门核心课程。本教材根据《普通高等院校本科外国语言文学类专业教学指南》，并结合普通高校英语专业的实际情况编写。本教材适用于英语专业、商贸专业、涉外文秘专业、旅游专业以及驻外机构人员培训等使用。

本书主要内容如下：

（1）根据目前普通高等院校英语专业翻译课的现状和学生的实际水平，本书以字词、词语、句子、段落和篇章为编写教材的主线，由浅入深、循序渐进，教师易讲解，学生易接受，能使教学效果最佳化。

（2）本书立足于基础知识，重点讲解翻译的基本理论以及翻译方法、技巧、艺术等。课文中的实例、译文赏析、讲解题和练习题也是从简单句到复杂句，便于学生理解、接受，能激发学生的学习兴趣。

（3）强调词语的选用、词语的搭配，并讲解多义词、成语、专有名词等的用法。

（4）讲解句子的主语和谓语以及其他成分，简单句和复合句的译法，句子结构重组，多种句型翻译，长句和难句译法等。

（5）篇章翻译的讲解中涵盖杂文、诗歌、小说、应用文，涉及科技类、商贸类等语篇。

本书主要特色如下：

（1）引导学生关注中英思维差异，养成良好的翻译习惯。

（2）选材多样，示例涵盖政治、经济、文化教育、文学、金融、商业、贸易、电商、互联网、大数据、物流、环境卫生、社会生活等，体现了新颖性、时代性、趣味性、实用性、科技性和综合性。

（3）秉持"精讲多练，重点突出，启发引导，由浅入深"的编写理念。每个章节先有理论论述，接着有实例列举，译文赏析，最后设置讲解题和练习题。

（4）为了便于教学，把讲解题和练习题的参考答案与课本分开，这样，教师有讲解的内容，学生能够集中精力听讲。课后，学生能够独立地完成练习。

本书由东南大学外国语学院梁为祥教授担任总主编，教育部高等院校英语专业教学指导委员会委员、扬州大学外国语学院院长王金铨教授担任主编，来自上海应用技术大学、安徽新华学院、绍兴文理学院、上海师范大学、扬州大学、东南大学等院校的专家和教师参加了本次修订工作。西安交通大学出版社领导和编辑的全力支持使得本教材顺利出版，在此一并表示感谢！

在编写过程中，难免会出现不妥之处，恳请广大师生和读者批评指正。

本教材配套参考答案，如有需要，请联系西安交通大学出版社，联系方式为：029-82665371。

编 者
2021.7

Contents

第 1 章　Summary of Translation（翻译概述） ·················001
 1.1　Criteria of Translation（翻译标准） ·················002
 1.2　Requirements for a Translator（对译者的要求） ·················002
 1.3　Strategies of Translation（翻译方法和步骤） ·················003

第 2 章　Translation Techniques of English Words Ⅰ
（英语词语翻译技巧Ⅰ） ·················007
 2.1　Selection and Extension of the Meaning of a Word
  （词义的选择与引申） ·················008
 2.2　Translation on Conversion of Parts of Speech
  （英语词性的转换与翻译） ·················019

第 3 章　Translation Techniques of English Words Ⅱ
（英语词语翻译技巧Ⅱ） ·················031
 3.1　Foreignization（异化翻译） ·················032
 3.2　Domestication（归化翻译） ·················033

第 4 章　Translation Techniques of English Words Ⅲ
（英语词语翻译技巧Ⅲ） ·················037
 4.1　Amplification in Translation（增词翻译） ·················038
 4.2　Omission in Translation（减词翻译） ·················045
 4.3　Repetition in Translation（重复翻译） ·················056

第 5 章　English Syntax and Translation（英语句法与翻译）·········065

- 5.1　Brief Introduction（简述） ···066
- 5.2　Differences between English and Chinese and Translation
（英汉句子的差异与译法） ···066
- 5.3　Translation on Negative Meaning in English Sentences
（英语句子否定意义的译法） ···072
- 5.4　Translation of Attributive Clauses and Adverbial Clauses
（定语从句和状语从句的翻译） ·····································080
- 5.5　Translation of Similar English Sentences
（英语相似句子的译法） ···085
- 5.6　Translation of Special English Sentences
（英语特殊句型的翻译） ···087
- 5.7　Translation of English Relative Clauses
（英语关系分句的译法） ···097
- 5.8　Translation of Long and Difficult Sentences in English
（英语长句和难句的译法） ···103

第 6 章　Literal and Free Translation in English
（直译法与意译法）···111

- 6.1　Literal Translation（直译）···112
- 6.2　Free Translation（意译） ···120
- 6.3　Literal and Free Translation of Practical Writings
（几种实用文体的直译和意译） ·····································126

第 7 章　Cultural Consciousness in English-Chinese Translation
（英译汉中的文化意识）···139

- 7.1　Differences in Cultural Consciousness（文化意识的差异）···140
- 7.2　Techniques of Translating English into Chinese on Difference
in Cultural Consciousness（文化意识差异的英译汉技巧）···148

第 8 章　**Translation of Discourse（语篇翻译）**··························157

    8.1　Translation of Literary Writings（文学语篇翻译）············158

    8.2　Translation of Scientific Writings（科技语篇的翻译）·········189

    8.3　Translation on Practical Writings（应用文语篇的翻译）······198

    8.4　Translation on Business and Trade Discourses in English
（商贸英语语篇的翻译）　···209

第 1 章

Summary of Translation
（翻译概述）

1.1　Criteria of Translation（翻译标准）

翻译的标准概括起来三个字——"信、达、雅",这也是衡量翻译质量好坏的一把尺子。简单地说,"信"就是译文能抓住源语的要旨,忠实于原文的意思;"达"要求译文语言规范、表达流畅、意思准确;"雅"指译文语言得体、简明优雅。具体来说,翻译标准有下列几点。

①译文的内容要反映出原文作者的思想、观点、立场和所流露的感情。

②译文要通顺达意,不拘泥于原文。

③译文要体现出原文的风格,特别是原作者的语言风格等。

一篇好的翻译作品必须做到既忠实于原文的意思,又体现出原文的风格。翻译时不可以逐词死译、生搬硬套,要符合语言的规范。可以说,忠实和通顺是衡量译文最重要的标准。

1.2　Requirements for a Translator（对译者的要求）

翻译工作质量的高低会直接影响到外事交流工作。要成为一个称职的翻译工作者,必须具备以下几个条件。

①要有较高的母语水平。这样才能有好的译文。

②要有扎实的外语功底。要具备良好的外语理解能力和表达能力,要有丰富的外语语言知识,包括词汇、句型结构、语法知识、文体的语言风格等。

③要掌握翻译理论知识,能够运用恰当的翻译技巧,从而少走弯路,达到事半功倍的效果。

④要有面对翻译困难的准备和认真的态度。翻译是一项复杂、艰苦的工作。鲁迅先生在谈到翻译工作的甘苦时曾说过:"我向来总以为翻译比创作容易,因为至少是无须构想,但真的一译就会遇到难

关,比如,一个名词或动词,写不出,创作的时候可以回避,翻译上却不成,也还得想,一直弄得头昏眼花,好像在脑子里面摸一个急于要开箱子的钥匙,却没有。"鲁迅先生的这段话应引起每个翻译者的深思。

1.3 Strategies of Translation(翻译方法和步骤)

英汉两种语言存在很大差异。翻译不仅是两种语言文字的转换,还涉及不同文化的交流,具体处理时方法灵活多变。

1. 翻译方法

1)直译

直译基本上就是按照源语的语言表达顺序和字面意思翻译,忠实于原文的意思。例如:We will build our motherland into a great modern socialist country.(我们要把祖国建设成社会主义现代化强国。)。此句的译文基本上是按照原文的内容顺序直接翻译出来的,忠实于原文的意思,表达也很清楚。

2)意译

意译要求译文忠实于原文,语言表达通顺,但不拘泥于原文的语言结构和形式,同时可能译出了原文的引申之意。例如:He had about as much chance of getting a job as of being chosen mayor of a city.(他找到工作的可能简直微乎其微。)。His behavior would try the patience of Job.(连最有耐心的人也可能无法容忍他的行为。)。

3)归化

归化就是用目的语的文化意识和表达形式来替代源语中的文化意识和表达形式,特别是要用目的语中的形象、比喻、风格来替代源语中的形象、比喻和风格。例如:Jack is a fair-weather friend.(杰克是一个不能共患难的朋友。)。Seeing is believing.(百闻不如一见。)。He is given an inch and will take a mile.(他得寸进尺。)。She is a cat.(她是个胆小鬼。)。

4）异化

异化就是译文不仅要忠实地传达原文中"说了些什么",还要尽可能揭示原作中是"怎么说的",最大限度地再现原作在语言文化上的特有风格和表达形式。例如：One stone tills two birds.（一石击二鸟）。

翻译时选用归化还是异化,并没有一个固定的答案。无论选用何种方法,都应考虑：①译文应该完全地复写出原作的思想内容；②译文的语言风格和笔调应该与原作保持一致；③译文的语言表达形式应该与原作同样流畅通顺。

2. 翻译步骤

1）吃透原文

阅读、分析和理解原文是十分重要的,包括字词、词性、词类、词义、语序以及它们在不同的语言环境中不同意思的用法和转换。例如：It's like carrying coals to Newcastle.（这完全是多此一举。）纽卡斯尔是英国的煤都,译者必须了解这个背景信息和英语中约定俗成的用法,才能准确译出原文的意思。

2）把源语翻译成目的语

这个过程涉及思维的转换,从源语的思维转换为目的语的思维,形成文化意识和内容的跨越。具体地说,译者理解原文的意思之后,再进一步分析句子各个成分之间的关系,然后在综合上下文的意思之后,开始构思译文。

比如,翻译短句时,先确定主谓语,然后再找出其他修饰语,接着按照目的语的思维方式和表达习惯译出译文。例如：I had let it be known through the local grapevine that I needed a night watchman for the tea factory on the estate of which I was the manager .（我是种植园的经理,曾通过当地的"义务小广播"向外发布种植园茶叶加工厂要找一个守夜人的信息）。这是一个复合句,翻译时,首先要看清楚原文结构和句意,再根据目的语的思维方式和表达需要,按照目的语的表达习惯,把译文呈现出来。

3）重组目的语

重组的过程涉及词法、句法等的转换,也要考虑原文的语篇特点。

4）修改译文

修改对翻译来说也很关键。译文初稿出来之后，先放到一边，时隔几日之后再来阅读初稿，修正误译，补充新的内容。将译文搁置几日后，再来阅读、修改，仔细地校对之后再定稿，使译文准确无误。

第 2 章

Translation Techniques of English Words Ⅰ
（英语词语翻译技巧Ⅰ）

2.1 Selection and Extension of the Meaning of a Word（词义的选择与引申）

1. 词义的选择

为了使译文准确、流畅，译者应该努力寻找最适合表达原文含义的词语或词组。选词应该在充分理解源语的基础上进行。翻译过程中，有时候需要借助于字典，但字典不能够解决所有问题，因为有时候原文中的词义和目的语的词义不能完全对等。如果把某些英语单词或词组按词典上的意义直译过来，就会使译文晦涩生硬，难以理解，还可能引起误解。这时就要根据上下文的语境和目的语的需要来确定词义。以常用词"story"和"bare"为例，其基本含义是"故事"和"光秃秃的"。但是，当词性不一样，或上下文不一样的时候，对它们的翻译就完全不同。

story 的不同译法

（1）The story of the hero is extremely moving.

【译文】 这个英雄故事令人极为感动。

【评析】 句中的"story"是名词，此处译为"故事"。

（2）He storied about his age.

【译文】 他隐瞒年龄。

【评析】 本句中的"storied"是动词，意思是"隐瞒、讲故事"。

（3）They all tell the same story.

【译文】 他们都是这样说。

【评析】 本句中的"story"是名词，但翻译时并没有译成名词，而是转换了词性。

（4）He does like to write the story of his life.

【译文】 他很喜欢写自己的生活经历。

【评析】 本句中的"story"是名词，此处译为"经历"。

（5）These figures gave only part of the story.

【译文】 这些数字只不过说明了部分情况。

【评析】 本句的"story"是名词,此处译为"情况、情节"。

(6) We must make a long story short.

【译文】 我们应该长话短说。

【评析】 句中的"story"是名词,但不应译为"故事",而是根据句意,译为"长话短说"。

bare 的不同译法

(1) These soldiers were fighting the enemies with bare hands.

【译文】 那些战士们正在赤手空拳同敌人搏斗。

【评析】 句中的"bare"是形容词,意思是"赤裸的、不穿衣服的",此处"bare hands"译为"赤手空拳"。

(2) When taking the bus, we saw a bare hill through the glass window.

【译文】 乘车的时候,我们透过车窗就看到了光秃秃的小山。

【评析】 句中的"bare"为形容词,意思是"光秃秃的、寸草不生的"。

(3) He lives in a room of bare furniture.

【译文】 他住在一间没有任何家具的房间。

【评析】 这里的"bare"为形容词,意思是"空的、缺乏的、无装饰的"。

(4) As long as there is only a bare possibility, we will do our best to do it well.

【译文】 只要存在一点点可能性,我们都会尽力做好这件事。

【评析】 这里的"bare"为形容词,意思是"稀少的、微小的、仅有的、勉强的"。

(5) The old peasant is very honest, and dares to speak the bare truth.

【译文】 这位老农民老实忠厚,并且敢于说真话。

【评析】 此句中的"bare"为形容词,意思是"不掩饰的、直率的"。

可见,一词多性、一词多义的现象在英语中十分普遍。翻译时,词义的选择应从以下几点着手。

1)根据词性来判断词义

许多英语单词具有不同的词性,可作为名词、动词、形容词、副词等，这往往给词义的理解和翻译带来困难。翻译时，可以根据语法关系来辨别该词在句中的词性，以便准确地判断词义。例如：

（1）It's two meters high（high 为形容词）这东西有两米高。

（2）pay high（high 为副词）出高价

（3）hit an all-time high（high 为名词）创史上最高纪录

（4）net profit（net 为形容词）纯利润

（5）communication net（net 为名词）通信网

（6）net a fat profit（net 为动词）净赚一大笔钱

在句子中，可根据语法知识辨别词的类别和词义。例如：

（1）The money which he makes mainly provides food and clothes for his family.

【译文】 他赚的钱主要供给家人衣食，用来养家糊口。

【评析】 这句中的"provide"是谓语动词，从整个句子的意思来判断，应该是"提供、供给"的意思。

（2）The company provides a ship with radar equipment.

【译文】 这个公司在船只上装上雷达设备。

【评析】 根据整个句子的意思来判断，"provide"是谓语动词，常与"with"搭配使用，表示"为……装备、为……提供"。

（3）The agreement provides that the two sides shall meet once a month.

【译文】 协议规定双方每月会晤一次。

【评析】 此句中的"provide"是动词，在主句中当谓语，表示"规定、议定"的意思。

（4）The department of foreign affairs is providing for the entertainment of its guests.

【译文】 外事部门正在为招待客人做准备。

【评析】 根据句意判断，这里的动词"provide"充当谓语，和"for"搭配使用，表示"为……做准备"。

（5）I should like time to read the novel.

【译文】 我希望有时间读一读这本小说。

【评析】 like 常和 should、would 连用表示"希望、想"。

(6) He has his likes and dislikes.

【译文】 他有好恶。

【评析】 此句中的"likes"为名词,表示"喜爱、爱好"。

(7) Like enough, the suspect will turn up in the hotel near the railway station.

【译文】 那个嫌疑人很可能会出现在火车站附近的酒店里。

【评析】 like enough 的意思是"大概、可能",多用于口语当中。

2)根据词的搭配关系判定词义

任何一种语言都会形成固定的词组或常见搭配。词与词之间搭配关系不同,词义也就会不同。由于英语、汉语之间的种种差异,这些比较固定的说法,有时可以译成另一种语言,有时则不行。因此,翻译时必须注意两种语言间的搭配差异。以 old 与其他词语的搭配为例。

old age 老年/晚年　　　　　　old man 老人
look old 显得老态　　　　　　old wine 陈酒
old civilization 古老文明　　　old society 旧社会
the old year 刚过去的一年　　 old customs 旧风俗
old students 以前的学生　　　old clothes 旧衣服
old rags 破烂　　　　　　　　old story 老一套
old hand 老手　　　　　　　　old Harry 魔鬼

以上均是"形容词 old ＋名词"短语,可以发现,与不同的名词搭配,old 的词义也不尽相同。又如 own 和 pace 的搭配用法。

(1) Jack is own brother to Barry.

【译文】 杰克是巴里的亲兄弟。

【评析】 句中的"own"是形容词,表示"嫡亲"的时候,用 be own sb. to sb.,译为"……是……的亲人"。

(2) He calls these books his own.

【译文】 他声称这些书为自己所有。

【评析】 call sth. one's own 表示"……为自己所有"。

(3) He comes into his own because of his hard work.

【译文】 由于他的努力工作，他得到了人们的信任。

【评析】 come into one's own 表示"应得的信任、名誉"等。

(4) John has been holding his own under the hard conditions.

【译文】 约翰在这样艰苦的条件下，一直在坚守。

【评析】 句中的"hold one's own"为固定搭配用法，表示"坚守住"。

(5) She has a mind of her own.

【译文】 她颇有主见。

【评析】 句中的"…of one's own"为固定搭配，表示"属于某人自己的"。

(6) She always is at a good pace when taking a walk every time.

【译文】 她身体很强壮，每次散步时，总是走得相当快。

【评析】 句中的"pace"为名词，构成"at a good pace"搭配时，意思是"相当快地"。

(7) The construction of the national defense must keep pace with the economic development.

【译文】 国防建设应该与经济建设同步发展。

【评析】 句中的"pace"为名词，构成"keep pace with"，表示"……与……同步"。

(8) We can put the students through their pace by tests.

【译文】 我们通过多次测试就能检测出这些学生的能力。

【评析】 句中的"pace"为名词，构成"…put sb. through one's pace"固定搭配，表示"检测某人的本领或能力/掂量某人的斤两"。

3) 根据语境确定词义

上下文的语境对词义影响极大，很多英语单词即使弄清楚了它的词性，还要从多个义项中选定确切的词义。这就需要借助于上下文提供的各种线索和语境做出合理的分析、推理、判断，确保理解和表达的准确性。

(1) My first impression that she disliked me soon vanished. I could see

through that putting off expression she wore habitually that she actually enjoyed chatting with me.

【译文】 开始我觉得她不喜欢我,但这种印象很快就消失了。我发现,虽然她常常显得冷冰冰的,实际上还是乐意与我闲聊。

【评析】 句中的"putting off"为"敷衍、躲避"的意思,在此句中,根据上下文语境,译为"冷冰冰的",表示一个女子隐含的一种态度,表面上和心里想的不是一回事。

(2) Every president, I am sure, leaves the university poorer than he was when he went in.

【译文】 我相信,每一位校长在离开学校时,他的财产总是比刚进校时少了。

【评析】 本句不能译为"……总要比他刚进学校时贫穷",显然不符合原句语义,根据语境应该译成"他的财产总是比刚进校时少了",这样才符合原文的意思。

(3) Suddenly the line went limp. "I'm going back," said Smith. "We must have a break somewhere. Wait for me. I will be back in five minutes."

【译文】 引爆线突然耷拉下来。史密斯说:"我回去看看。一定是某个地方断了线。等一下,我五分钟就回来。"

【评析】 通常情况下,"have a break"的意思是"休息一下",但是在此句中,根据上文"suddenly the line went limp(引爆线突然耷拉下来)"判断,"have a break"表示"断了线"的意思。

(4) Nancy always gets what she wants by playing office politics.

【译文】 南希在办公室总是靠耍手腕来达到她的目的。

【评析】 "politics"的意思是"政治",是中性词,但在本句话中,应译成贬义词"耍手腕"才能与上下文意义呼应。

Versions for Appreciation(译文赏析)

(1) The operation only just succeeded and it was fortunate that we had provided additional medicine specialists.

【译文】 这个手术好不容易才取得成功，多亏我们增加了医学专家。

【评析】 原文中的"only just"如果不联系上下文理解其意，往往就被译成"刚刚"。根据上下文语境，"only just"在此句中表示一种语气，与时间没有关系，故"好不容易才"是最佳的译文。

（2）The environmental company has raised its JV equity to 60% to gain management control. It has trebled its initial investment and is now expanding its product range and manufacturing capacity to meet growing demands.

【译文】 这个环保公司将其在合资公司的股份增至60%，以获得管理控制权。这使它的先期投资增加了两倍，而且它现在正在扩大产品范围和生产能力来满足不断增长的需求。

【评析】 "equity"通常是"公正、公平"的意思，在金融术语中则用来指企业资产中各方所占的比例。"initial investment"是商贸英语中常用术语，意思是"先期投资"或"预付款"，不能直译为"一开始的投资"。

（3）It must be a terrific ego trip. He can't help but think people are for him.

【译文】 那一定是一次极好的自我表现的机会，他禁不住想人们是会支持他的。

【评析】 如果将原句译成"那一定是一次可怕的自我表现的机会。他禁不住想着人们是会支持他的"，就显得语句极不通顺，问题出在"可怕的自我表现的机会"，这样的表述无法令读者明白其意。根据"ego trip（自我表现的机会）"，以及后一句"He can't help but think people are for him.（他禁不住想着人们是会支持他的）"，将"terrific"译作"极好的"是最妥当的。

Questions for Teacher's Lecture（讲解题）

Translate the following sentences into Chinese.

（1）His mother had died when Yasha was seven and the father had not remarried; the boy had to raise himself.

(2) Take the cart back to the backyard and back it into the shed at the back of the stable.

(3) I can not stomach this job any longer.

(4) I can know her at once by her walk.

(5) He enjoys the company of intelligent girl, well learned men and his close friends.

(6) He claims to have been graduated from the college, but his name is not on the books.

(7) That's the basic problem, and there's a basic answer—firmness and clarity.

(8) He killed the proposal when it came from the committee.

(9) I will do everything within my power to assist you.

(10) Basically, all power is with the people.

(11) The terms of the transaction have been negotiated on an arm's length basis.

Exercises for Students（练习题）

Translate the following sentences into Chinese.

(1) While these underprivileged people get help from the organization, they have no high hopes for their future.

(2) In the business college students are taught to keep books.

(3) The margins for the services business come to only 14 percent.

(4) The night watchman makes his rounds every hour.

(5) The manager addressed shareholders prior to the company's merger with a Swedish company.

(6) In an attempt to address this problem, major banks are about to offer start-up packages to assist new business.

2. 词义的引申

翻译时，应根据语境以及逻辑关系，从词语的本义出发，进行恰当、合理的引申。词义引申是建立在合理联想的基础之上，与词语本义有着紧密联系。翻译时，首先要弄清原文的意思和词语的本义，然后按照汉语表达习惯，选择适当的词义加以引申，以求表意更加确切，但不能脱离原文词义的基本范畴。词义引申通常从下面几点着手。

1）抽象化到具体化的翻译

根据汉语表达习惯，将词义引申为意义较明确的词，将抽象的词义具体化，使译文表达清晰、准确、流畅。

（1）Parents can do a tremendous amount to help their kids learn to read, but pushing them before they're ready can backfire.

【译文】 父母可以做大量的事情帮助孩子们学会看书，但若超过孩子的智力和愿望，强迫他们学习，反而适得其反。

【评析】 此句中的 "before they're ready" 比较抽象，如果将它译成 "准备不足或准备好之前"，译文不清晰，只有译成 "超过孩子们的智力和愿望"，意思才具体。

（2）The day is long gone when the oil-company profits transformed the proud new skylines of New Orleans and Houston into testaments to a time of plenty.

【译文】 石油公司的利润曾使新奥尔良和休斯敦的城市面貌彻底地改观，高楼大厦林立，城市骄傲地炫耀繁荣富足，但那种日子早已成为过眼云烟。

【评析】 句子中的 "...transformed the proud of new skylines of..." 从字面上译有些抽象，译成 "高楼大厦林立，城市骄傲地炫耀着……" 比较具体，表意明确。

（3）He had surfaced with less visibility in the policy decisions.

【译文】 在决策过程中，他已经不那么抛头露面了。

【评析】 句中的 "less visibility" 译为 "极少可见，极少能见度"，意思抽象，不明确，翻译成 "抛头露面" 意思清晰。

(4) All the irregularities of the students in that university resulted in punishment.

【译文】 在那所大学里，有越轨行为的学生都受到了处罚。

【评析】 句中的"irregularities"表示抽象概念，若译为"不规则、不规律的事物"，表意不具体。所以，将其译成"越轨行为"比较具体，也与处罚的意思相吻合。

2）具体化到抽象化的翻译

英语中有很多的形象化的比喻和习语，也有很多的词语由于多种原因无法移植到汉语中来，这时候，就需要"舍形取义"，也就是从具体化向抽象化转换。有时候，翻译时还需要加注，更好地将词义从具体引申为抽象，从特殊引向一般，从局部引向概括等。

(1) Scotland's beaches once again passed European Union water quality tests with flying colors.

【译文】 苏格兰的海滩再次成功通过了欧盟的水质监测。

【评析】 "with flying colors"原指凯旋的船队驶回本国港口时，桅杆上挂满彩旗，此处可引申为"凯旋""大功告成"。

(2) I'm afraid she's too far from the cradle for you.

【译文】 她对你来说恐怕岁数太大了。

【评析】 句中的"too far from the cradle"具体的意思是"离儿时太远"，译为抽象化的意思"岁数太大了"，符合汉语表达习惯。

Versions for Appreciation（译文赏析）

(1) Although the merger of "dot" and "com" has created so many young millionaires, there is a new topic: venture capital.

【译文】 尽管网络公司的兼并造就了如此多的百万富翁，但我们面临一个新的话题：风险资本。

【评析】 "dot"和"com"是常见的域名后缀，意思是"network company"，翻译时有必要将它们引申为"网络公司"，既符合原文语义，也易于中文读者接受。

（2）Shenzhen has entered the league of the most promising emerging markets.

【译文】 深圳已经成为最具有前途的新兴市场之一。

【评析】 句中的"entered the league"字面意思是"进入联盟"，在这个句子里，译为"成为最具前途的新兴市场"符合句意。

Questions for Teacher's Lecture（讲解题）

Translate the following sentences into Chinese.

（1）How do we account for this split between the critics and the readers, the head and the heart?

（2）When he was young he quitted his hometown and traveled to the capital, which he reached in a state of almost utter destitution.

（3）The will and wisdom of a man determine his future destiny.

（4）It is a silly fish that is caught twice with the same bait.

（5）For a good hour, we talk of our life, our ambition and our future.

（6）Let us revise our safety and sanitary regulations in school.

Exercises for Students（练习题）

Translate the following sentences into Chinese.

（1）The president's speech covered the history of Chinese examination system, the current situation of education and how to take a right attitude to examination.

（2）His business mushroomed when he opened the new store.

（3）No one should claim infallibility.

（4）For the balance of the section, let's speak in straightforward and elementary terms to describe the function and form of the electronic computer.

（5）They attended the meeting despite the rain and catching cold.

（6）We have to analyze and solve problems when we meet some difficulties.

2.2　Translation on Conversion of Parts of Speech（英语词性的转换与翻译）

　　由于英汉两种语言在形态、结构和表达的手法上存在着很大的差异，直接用汉语按照英语的形态与结构把原文的意思再现出来的情况并不多。在大多数情况下，要进行词性的转换和词序的调整，即把英语的某一类词转换成汉语的另一类词，这样才能使译文既忠于原文又符合汉语习惯和语法规则。词性转换有以下几种。

1. 英语名词译为汉语动词

　　这种转化主要有两种形式：英语动词的派生词转化成汉语动词，如formation、growth、swimmer、estimation等；具有动词词性或动词含义的英语名词转化成汉语动词，如cheer、victory、approach等。

　　（1）The new situation requires the formation of a new strategy.

　　【译文】　新形势要求制定新战略。

　　【评析】　"formation"在句中用作名词，译成汉语时，转换为动词"制定"。

　　（2）We should take full use of advantage of this opportunity to push the sales of our products.

　　【译文】　我们应该充分利用此机会进行产品促销。

　　【评析】　"use"在原文中是名词，在译文中译成动词"利用"。

　　（3）China is one of the earliest cradles of civilization and a visit to this ancient civilization country has long been my dream.

　　【译文】　中国是最古老的文明摇篮之一，访问这个文明古国是我多年梦寐以求的愿望。

　　【评析】　本句中的"visit"是一个具有动词意义的名词，汉译时往往需要转译为动词。

（4）China's stable economic growth and increasingly improved social facilities have brought travelers much convenience.

【译文】 中国经济稳健增长，社会设施日益完善，这也给游客出行带来诸多的方便。

【评析】 "growth"在原文中用作名词，在译文中译成"增长"，为动词。

（5）For these years, I have been a much better swimmer than my wife.

【译文】 这些年来，我游泳一直都比我的妻子要好得多。

【评析】 "swimmer"在这里并不表达一个具体的身份或职业。为了使译文流畅，往往需要将这一类的名词转化成汉语动词。

（6）We must be of good cheer for his achievement.

【译文】 我们应该为他的成就而高兴。

【评析】 "cheer"在原文中是名词，在译文中转换为动词，意思是"为……而高兴"。

2. 英语形容词译为汉语动词

在英语中，有很多形容词并不做修饰语，而是与系动词组成谓语，表示某种意愿、态度，以及感知、情感和欲望等心理状态，并且通过介词连接宾语。英译汉时通常把英文里的形容词转换为中文中的动词。

（1）The American entrepreneurs hailed the program for greater Sino-US trade.

【译文】 美国企业家们对这个扩大中美贸易的计划表示欢迎。

【评析】 "greater"在原文里是形容词，在译文中转换为动词，意思是"扩大"。

（2）Fair treatment of China by its trading partners could lead to a new era of cooperation and warmer relations on all levels between China and other WTO members.

【译文】 贸易伙伴如果都能公平对待中国，将有利于中国和其他世贸组织成员进入一个改善关系、全面合作的时期。

【评析】 "warmer"在原文里是形容词，在译文中转换为动词，译为

"改善"。

（3）His ill health has been a very anxious business.

【译文】 他的身体不好，使人十分担心。

【评析】 原文中"anxious"为形容词，转换为译文中的动词，译为"担心"。

3. 英语复合谓语译为汉语动词

英文中表示心理状态的形容词与系动词构成的复合谓语，翻译时一般转换成汉语动词。

英语中有许多表示知觉、情感、欲望、意愿、态度、感受、信念等心理状态的形容词，例如：useful、helpful、eatable、dangerous、harmless、available、angry、able、afraid、ashamed、aware、anxious、careful、cautious、certain、concerned、confident、doubtful、envious、embarrassed、glad、grateful、ignorant、jealous、sorry、thankful等，当这些形容词与前面的系动词一起描述主语的某种状态时，通常需要将类似的形容词转换成汉语动词。

（1）He is very angry at his failure in this experiment.

【译文】 他对这次实验的失败感到非常生气。

【评析】 句中的"angry"是形容词，和系动词"is"一起连用，构成"is very angry"，在句中用作动词复合谓语，表示一种心理状态，汉译时转换为动词"对……感到生气"。

（2）Tom is ignorant of the duties he undertakes in marrying.

【译文】 汤姆完全不懂他在婚姻方面应承担的责任。

【评析】 句中的"ignorant"和前面的系动词构成谓语动词，描述主语的状态，汉译时转化为动词"不明白、不懂得"。

（3）John is really sorry for his past，and he has undertaken to give up cars entirely and for ever.

【译文】 约翰对过去追悔莫及，并保证永远不开汽车。

【评析】 句中的"sorry"为形容词，和系动词"is"连用，构成动词复合谓语，意为"感到后悔"，表现一种心理状态。

（4）The manager is hopeful that he can continue our meeting with these people.

【译文】 这位经理希望能继续与这些人会晤。

【评析】 句中的"is hopeful"与系动词"is"连用,转译成动词复合谓语,译为"希望"。

4. 英语介词译为汉语动词

英语中介词很多,例如:in、on、of、off、about、into、beyond、to、over、against、by、with 等。这些介词中,有些含有动词意味,翻译时也常常转换为汉语动词。此外还有动词的现在分词做介词,例如:concerning、regarding 等。同样还有很多的介词短语,例如:in according with、according to、in view of、owing to、on account of、at the cost of、at the price of、beyond expression、beyond question、by means of、by way of、for the sake of、on behalf of、under discussion 等。在很多情况下,翻译介词和介词短语也可以转换成汉语动词或动词词组。

(1) We believe that the normalization of relations between the two countries is not only in the interest of the Chinese and American peoples, but also contributes to the relaxation of tension in Asia and the world.

【译文】 我们相信,两国关系正常化不仅符合中美两国人民利益,而且将对缓和亚洲和世界紧张局势做出贡献。

【评析】 原文中"in"为介词,在译文里转换为动词,译为"符合"。

(2) All the leaders and fighters among the Red Army worked long hours on meager food, in cold caves, by dim lamps.

【译文】 所有红军领导和战士们吃着粗茶淡饭,住着冰凉的窑洞,点着昏暗的油灯,长时间地工作着。

【评析】 原文中的三个介词"on""in""by"分别转译为汉语动词"吃""住""点",译文简洁、准确。

(3) The man is very wise, and he can see beyond the simple happenings to their farthest implication.

【译文】 这个人很聪明,他能透过简单的事件看到其最深远的含义。

【评析】 原文中的介词"beyond"转译为汉语动词"透过"。

（4）This company is turning China for capital and technology.

【译文】 这家公司正在转向中国寻求资金和技术。

【评析】 句中的介词"for"在译文中转译为动词"寻求"。

Versions for Appreciation（译文赏析）

（1）A very little encouragement would set that wordy woman to talk volubly, and poured out all within her.

【译文】 只要大家稍稍助助她的兴，这个庸俗的女人就会立刻滔滔不绝地把一肚子话和盘托出。

【评析】 "encouragement"是动词"encourage"的派生词，有较强的动作意义，根据汉语表达习惯，将它转译为动词"助兴"，同时将形容词"little"转译为副词"稍稍"。

（2）All people are deeply convinced that the policy of this country will have a positive impact on our bilateral and multilateral relations.

【译文】 大家都深信，这个政策将对我们的双边和多边关系产生积极的影响。

【评析】 "convinced"与系动词"are"共同构成谓语动词，描述主语"all people"的心理状态，汉译时转译为动词"相信"。译文准确地传递了原文的意思。

（3）He is a worker with both consciousness and culture.

【译文】 他是一个有觉悟、有文化的劳动者。

【评析】 本句中的介词"with"具有动词意味，汉译时转译成动词"具有"，恰如其分地传达出原文的意思。

（4）The car goes eastward, across an avenue, by little shops and meat market, past single storied homes, until suddenly it stops against a wide green lawn.

【译文】 这辆车向东而去，穿过一条大街，经过了几家店铺和肉市，又越过了几幢平房，最后突然停在一片开阔的绿草坪前。

【评析】 该句中有五个介词，分别是"across""by""past""until""a

gainst"，在权衡原文的含义、汉语的搭配方式以及表达习惯的基础上，将它们分别翻译为"穿过""经过""越过""直到"和"在……前"，行文一气呵成，准确流畅。

5. 英语动词、形容词译为汉语名词

英语中有些动词，尤其是名词派生而来的动词，在翻译时往往转换成名词。

1）英语动词译为汉语名词

英语中有些动词的概念，难以直接用汉语动词来表达，这时可以转换成汉语名词。

（1）Trade union leaders claimed that some of their members had been victimized by being dismissed.

【译文】 工会领袖们认为有些会员遭到解雇，成了牺牲品。

【评析】 句中的"victimized"为动词谓语，在译文里转换为名词"牺牲品"。

（2）On average, LG shoppers spend ＄110 per order, triple what US TV shoppers spend.

【译文】 LG 的顾客每次订货的平均消费是 110 美元，为美国电视购物者一次平均消费额的 3 倍。

【评析】 动词"spend"汉译时转化为名词"消费"，译文妥帖、简洁。

（3）Today, the audience attending the meeting laughed the lecturer down.

【译文】 今天，出席会议的听众用讪笑声把演讲者轰下了台。

【评析】 "laughed"在原文中为谓语动词，在译文里转换成名词"讪笑"。

（4）With a few seconds，the meter needle should read zero.

【译文】 在几秒钟内，表中的读数应为零。

【评析】 原句动词"read"转化为汉语名词"读数"，符合科技用语表达习惯。

2）英语形容词译为汉语名词

英语定冠词 the 用在名词化的形容词或过去分词前，表示某一类人

或事物，相当于汉语中的名词"……人/者/员/物"。这类常见的形容词有 the sick、the elderly、the young、the old、the rich、the poor、the wounded、the new、the industrious、the false unemployed 等。

（1）A voice controlled device is a convenience for the elderly and it may become indispensable for a wide variety of chores in the home.

【译文】 声控装置能提供方便，对于老年人来说，它可能成为他们从事各种家庭杂事不可缺少的帮手。

【评析】 "the elderly"在本句话中译为"老年人"。

（2）The wounded are successful in undertaking by his own efforts.

【译文】 这位伤者凭借他自己的努力获得事业的成功。

【评析】 "the wounded"为形容词，译文中转化为名词"伤者"。

（3）The life of the unemployed, in America, becomes harder with the soaring of prices of various goods.

【译文】 随着各种商品价格飞涨，美国失业者的生活变得越加艰难。

【评析】 形容词"the unemployed"转换为名词"失业人员"。

6. 英语副词、名词转换成汉语形容词

在英语中，有不少副词是从形容词或名词派生而来的，因此在译成汉语时，可酌情将副词和名词转换为形容词。

1）副词译为汉语形容词

（1）Through many experiments, it has been demonstrated that gases are perfectly elastic.

【译文】 很多次实验已证实了气体具有理想的弹性。

【评析】 形容词"elastic"转换成名词"弹性"，副词"perfectly"转换为形容词"理想的"。

（2）The experiments have proved that earthquakes are closely related to faulting.

【译文】 实验已证明地震与断裂运动有着密切的关系。

【评析】 副词"closely"在原句中修饰过去分词"related"，在译文中转换为形容词"密切的"。

（3）We all know that advertising affects tremendously every sphere of modern life.

【译文】 我们都知道广告对现代生活的方方面面产生极大的影响。

【评析】 副词"tremendously"转换为形容词"极大的"。

（4）The official routinely radioed another agent on the ground.

【译文】 这位军官跟另一个地勤人员进行了例行的无线电联络。

【评析】 副词"routinely"转换成形容词"例行的"。

2）英语名词译为汉语形容词

翻译英语中从形容词派生出来的名词往往可以转译成汉语形容词。

（1）As the student is a newcomer, I hope you will give him the necessary help.

【译文】 因为这位学生是新来的，我希望你们能给他必要的帮助。

【评析】 名词"newcomer"在译文中转译为汉语形容词"新来的"。

（2）The author has overdrawn the villain to the point of absurdity.

【译文】 作者把那个反面人物夸张到了荒唐的地步。

【评析】 名词"absurdity"在译文中转换为形容词，译为"荒唐的"。

（3）The fair price connected with the superiority of varieties of our products will be able to guarantee our competitive edge in the international market.

【译文】 我方各种各样的产品价格公平，品质优良，能够确保在国际市场有竞争优势。

【评析】 名词"superiority"是由形容词"superior"派生而来，汉译时转译为形容词"优良的"。

7. 英语形容词译为汉语副词

英语中的名词转换为汉语的动词时，修饰这个名词的形容词相应地转换为汉语的副词。

（1）Especial care should be taken when handling flammable materials.

【译文】 使用易燃材料时一定要特别地小心。

【评析】 "care"转换成了动词"小心"，形容词"especial"转换为副词，译为"特别地"。

（2）Perhaps she would prod at the straw in her clumsy impatience.

【译文】 也许她会迫不及待地、笨手笨脚地翻弄那个草铺。

【评析】 "clumsy impatience"是移就格。"clumsy"和"impatience"分别修饰谓语"prod at"，形容词"clumsy"转换为副词，译为"笨手笨脚地"。

（3）Sellers should take full use of advantage of this opportunity to push the sales of our products.

【译文】 销售人员应当充分地利用此机会进行产品促销。

【评析】 原文中的形容词"full"转译为副词"充分地"，修饰动词短语"take use of"。

Versions for Appreciation（译文赏析）

（1）His poems are characterized by good lingering charm and bright colors.

【译文】 他的诗特点是韵味十足，色彩鲜明。

【评析】 动词"characterized"由名词"character"派生而来，汉译时将其转译为名词"特点"，语言简练、达意。

（2）John would no sooner send his old mother to the home for the aged than let her stay at home alone.

【译文】 约翰不会把年迈的母亲送到养老院，正如不会把她独自一人留在家里一样。

【评析】 定冠词"the"与形容词"aged"一起使用表达一类人，此处是指"老人"，"the home for the aged"译为"养老院"。

（3）Maliya impressed her fiancé's relatives favorably with her beauty.

【译文】 玛利亚的美丽给她未婚夫的亲戚们留下了极好的印象。

【评析】 该句中的动词"impress"转译为汉语中的名词"印象"，修饰"impress"的副词"favorably"相应转译成形容词"极好的"，以符合汉语表达方式。

Questions for Teacher's Lecture（讲解题）

Translate the following sentences into Chinese.

（1）He admires the President's stated decision to fight for the job.

（2）The international food shortage had a direct impact on some barren desert countries.

（3）Doctors have said that they are not sure they can save his life.

（4）The man ran back down into the cellar.

（5）After a short pause, they continued walking.

（6）A few steps across the lawn brought me to a large and splendid hotel.

（7）We are aiming in this period to teach recognition of the topic sentence as quickly as possible.

（8）Your work is characterized by lack of attention to detail.

（9）He is physically weak but mentally sound.

（10）Traditionally, there had always been good relations between these two countries.

（11）Independent observers have commented favorably on the achievements you have made in this direction.

（12）I am sorry I wasn't in when you rang me up.

Exercises for Students（练习题）

Translate the following sentences into Chinese.

（1）The fact that she was able to send a message was a hint. But I had to be cautious.

（2）An acquaintance with world history is helpful to the study of current situation.

（3）"Coming!" Away she skimmed over the lawn, up the path, up the steps, across the veranda, and into the porch.

（4）Computers mean so much in our life that without it our life would be unimaginable.

（5）On that day they were escorted to the Great Wall of China.

（6）I found him at his book when I came into the room.

（7）He seems quite suitable for the position because of his wide experience and success in similar jobs.

第 3 章

Translation Techniques of English Words II
（英语词语翻译技巧 II）

异化与归化是翻译中的两种策略，最早由美国翻译理论学家劳伦斯·韦努蒂于1995年在《译者的隐身》一书中提出。

3.1 Foreignization（异化翻译）

译文不仅要忠实地传达原作"说了什么内容"，而且还要尽可能地展示出原作是"怎么说的"，以便使译文最大限度地再现原作在语言和文化上的特有风格。

（1）Time is money.

【译文】 时间就是金钱。

【评析】 "时间就是金钱"的译文保留了原文的结构，比"一寸光阴一寸金"使用更普遍。

（2）Playwrights and playboys share space with those players who, having made in San Francisco or Fort Worth, simply need a bigger playing field. "New York is the social Olympics," as one commentator puts it. "The rest are just try outs."

【译文】 剧作家和花花公子们与许多其他社会名流平分秋色。虽然这些名流都已经在旧金山或沃斯堡提高了知名度，但仍需找个更大的扬名之地。一位评论家说："纽约才是社交圈的奥运会，其他的只能算是热身赛。"

【评析】 该句使用转喻。纽约是精英荟萃之地，奥运会则以竞争激烈而著称，因此译为"社交圈的奥运会"可以把纽约那种竞争激烈但又能提升个人价值的含义淋漓尽致地表达出来。

Questions for Teacher's Lecture（讲解题）

Translate the following sentences into Chinese.

（1）For realizing our goals, we should make effective use of various resources.

(2) Our country has been vigorously carrying forward the renovation of large transportation project.

(3) Today, the report on "Internet System" is made by a computer software engineer.

(4) There has been a big increase in the total volume of import and export in our province.

Exercises for Students(练习题)

Translate the following sentences into Chinese.

(1) Your exhibits are very attractive. The designs are very original. I'm sure many of the exhibits here will find a ready market in my country.

(2) In his temperament as in the circumstance of his time, he was destined for an extraordinary career.

(3) Now it is nine o'clock and you two TV watchers haven't done reading yet, on the double.

(4) China's stable economic growth and increasingly improved social facilities have brought travelers much convenience.

(5) It is that country's goal that the people in the undeveloped areas will be finally off poverty by the end of 2020 year.

3.2　Domestication（归化翻译）

在翻译过程中，如果没有办法用异化翻译的策略，可以使用归化翻译，应充分考虑自己的译文是否符合目的语的语言和文化规范。例如：

(1) ...for, consider, it was for one minute that she had left school, and the impressions of six years are not got over in that space of time.

【译文】　你想，她刚刚跨出校门一分钟，六年来受到的教诲，哪里能在这么短短的一刹那给忘掉呢？

【评析】 句中的"impression"的释义是"印象"，如果直接译为"六年得到的印象"会让读者感到译文不地道。按照汉语的表达习惯，用归化法把"impression"译成"教诲"就会非常贴切。

（2）50% the population are living in cities and towns.

【译文】 城镇化率达到百分之五十。

【评析】 英译汉中，要注意"具体转为宏观"的翻译原则。所以，英译汉时不必完全受制于英语的思维方式和行文特点，而应跳脱出来，进行脱壳（deverbalize）处理。本句就是用了归化法把句子翻译出来，符合汉语的表达习惯。

Questions for Teacher's Lecture（讲解题）

Translate the following sentences into Chinese.

（1）We sat down, and after a while a voice of unmistakable authority called, "Send in the new applicant".

（2）If companies want to tout such random, unaudited watch-me-pull-a-rabbit-out-of-my-hat figures in their press, well, fine.

（3）The decline of the dollar does, however, has a silver lining. U.S. exports will become cheaper and this will not only help restrain the deterioration in the trade balance over the next two years but will also help boost U.S. economy as a whole.

（4）The trade deficit on the total current will remain billions of dollars as far as the eye can see.

（5）The kaleidoscope of shifting interests of the nation during the negotiation made it impossible to sort out the "winners" and the "losers".

Exercises for Students（练习题）

Translate the following sentences into Chinese.

（1）If you want me to serve you, oh God, reveal yourself, perform a miracle, let your voice be heard.

（2）He would be imprisoned in a room at night with the lock clamped on the outside of the door, and the next morning he would be seen nonchalantly strolling through the market place.

（3）"... I don't hate to hear you swearing at your little boy, with that peculiar whine in your voice. Don't—please don't tear your clothes so savagely."

第 4 章

Translation Techniques of English Words III
（英语词语翻译技巧 III）

4.1 Amplification in Translation（增词翻译）

增词法是常用的英汉翻译手段之一，是指在原文的基础上添加必要的语言成分。增词绝不是无中生有，而是出于翻译效果的需要，通过增加原文中虽无其词却有其意的词、词组或句子，使译文在意义或结构上具有完整性，在语法、语言形式上符合汉语习惯。例如：

arrangement（安排情况）　　flexibility（灵活的态度）
solution（解决办法）　　　　inequality（不平等现象）
dislike（厌恶情绪）　　　　　divorce（离婚率）
tension（紧张局势）　　　　　management（管理工作）
arrogance（傲慢态度）　　　　loftiness（崇高气质）
necessity（必要性）　　　　　foolhardiness（蛮干作风）
jealousy（嫉妒心理）　　　　 preparation（准备工作）
complexity（复杂局面）　　　 madness（疯狂行为）
complacency（自满情绪）

下面就一些常用的增词法进行归纳、举例。

1. 使译文句法完整

增词是翻译中一种常用、有效的补充语义的手段。通常情况下，译者可根据句子的结构、意思、修辞等，在译文中适当地增加词语，补足语言转换后缺失的含义，使译文完整、通顺，再现原文真实的意义和风格。

（1）The sightseeing and tourism benefit not only airlines, hotels, restaurants, and taxi drivers, among others, but also many commercial establishments and even the manufacturers of tourist commodities.

【译文】 观光业和旅游业不仅有利于航空公司、酒店、餐饮、出租车等行业，而且还有利于许多商业机构，甚至有利于生产旅游商品的制造业。

【评析】 原文中谓语动词"benefit"后跟了若干个名词做宾语，若照搬同样结构，译文会显得生硬。重复"有利于"使译文句法完整，行文紧凑。

（2）We must know the Internet, how it works and how people use it. Google is all about inventing new ways of finding the information you want.

【译文】 我们应该知道因特网，知道它是如何运作的，知道人们是如何使用它的。谷歌就是用新的办法来找到你所需要的东西。

【评析】 重复动词是增词法中常用的一种手段。译文中增加了两次"知道"，使句子层次清晰，语义通顺，易读易懂。

（3）Innovation can make our products upgrade and creates a true competitive advantage.

【译文】 创新可以使我们的产品升级，创新可以使我们具有真正的竞争优势。

【评析】 译文重复"创新"，明晰了两个小句之间的并列关系，读起来朗朗上口，颇具气势，增强了语句的表现力。

2. 增加解释性的辅助动词，使译文符合汉语表达习惯

译者在翻译时往往需要解释原文中有关内容的背景情况，使读者更好地理解原文，翻译可在译文里适当地增词或引申，达到解释的目的。

（1）We need the courage and determination to further free our mind in order to make new breakthroughs in the reform of the economic and political systems.

【译文】 我们需要鼓足勇气，下定决心，解放思想，来取得经济和政治体系改革的新突破。

【评析】 如果将"We need the courage and determination to further..."按原句结构译成"我们需要勇气和决心……"，语气平淡，缺乏气势。增加"鼓足"和"下定"两个动词后，搭配协调，更加彰显出讲话者的魄力、坚定和信心。

（2）The manager spoke hopefully of the success of the business negotiation.

【译文】 经理满怀希望地谈到商务谈判会取得成功。

【评析】 译文增加了动词"取得",使行文顺畅、自然。

(3) There are problems with each of these ways; but at least they're a step in the right direction.

【译文】 这些方法都有各自的利弊,但至少都朝着正确的方向迈出了一步。

【评析】 译文增加辅助动词"迈出",使其通顺、完整。

3. 增加原文中隐含的某些词,从而把隐含意义表达出来

原文中往往有很多词语或句子富有隐含的意思,字面上没有体现出来。翻译时,译者可根据原文的本义以及译文的表达需要,增加一些词语把隐含的意思表达出来。

(1) At a large terminal railway station, the work of the stationmaster is largely administrative because of the extent of the operations and the staff of which he is in command.

【译文】 在大的铁路终点站,站长的工作主要是行政管理性的,这是由于车站运营范围广、工作人员多。

【评析】 译文增加了"广"和"多"两个词,将原文中未说透的意思明白无误地表达出来,使原句隐含的意思变得清楚、完整。

(2) The clever girl became a poor third in the English-speaking contest.

【译文】 这位聪明的女孩在英语演讲比赛中获得了第三名,成绩比第二名差了很多。

【评析】 原文乍看简单,但"poor third"值得琢磨。译文增加"成绩比第二名差了很多"不失为成功的手笔。

(3) Our company would like to quote our new customers the most reasonable price to start our business relationship for the future, even at the cost of a substantial loss on our part.

【译文】 为了推动我们未来业务的发展,我们公司愿意给新客户以最公道的价格,即使这样做会使我方蒙受相当大的损失,我们也在所不惜。

【评析】 原文"at the cost of a substantial loss on our part"结构简练,

却含义丰富。汉译时，需要将其背后的意思充分挖掘出来，增加"即使这样做会使我方蒙受相当大的损失，我们也在所不惜"后就把句中的隐含意思翻译出来了。

4. 增加语气词，再现原文语气

英语中有很多词语和句子都有隐含的语气。汉语中也有很多的语气词，例如：啦、啊、呢、呀、吗、吧、罢了等，分别表示不同的语气和感情色彩。翻译时，应根据译文的需要，适当地增加语气词。

（1）The beautiful girl on the cover of the periodical is just a sales gimmick.

【译文】 画报的封面上印上美女只不过是吸引顾客的一种噱头而已。

【评析】 汉语中的语气有时需要靠语气词本身来体现。译文通过增加语气词"不过……而已"体现了原文本要表达的内在含义和语气。

（2）Don't take it seriously. I'm just joking.

【译文】 不要当真嘛，我只是开个玩笑啦。

【评析】 译文中增加了两个语气词"嘛"和"啦"，把原句中的语气完全再现了出来。

（3）Maybe her real basic weakness might be some form of kindness.

【译文】 说不定她真正的根本弱点就在于某种形式的仁慈吧。

【评析】 译文增加的语气词"说不定……吧"恰当地表现出原文中副词"maybe"和情态动词"might"的确切含义。

（4）Through tests, the doctor told me that there must be a family history of seizures and that I just didn't know about it.

【译文】 经过检查之后，医生告诉我说，一定是有家族疾病病史，我只是不知道罢了。

【评析】 增加的语气词"……罢了"忠实地体现出原文中"must be"和"just"的语义内涵。

5. 增加数词或表示多数含义的词

英语中有些表示数量概念的词语是模糊的，不用具体数字来表示。翻译时，可用增加数词的方式或其他语言表达的形式把原文的数字概念清楚地表达出来。

(1) They persisted in their reform in spite of the difficulties.

【译文】 尽管困难重重，他们仍坚持改革。

【评析】 汉语中名词没有复数形式，可通过增加叠词"重重"呼应原文中的复数概念。

(2) In our work we often have to analyze and solve problems.

【译文】 在我们的工作中，我们常常要分析一些问题，要解决一些问题。

【评析】 原文中的"problems"是复数形式，但汉语中的"问题"没有复数形式，可以通过增加表示多数含义的词把原文中的复数形式表达出来。不过有时候"一些"也可省略不译。

(3) I have heard such stories, so I won't listen to another.

【译文】 我已听过许多这样的故事，所以不愿意再听了。

【评析】 原文中的"stories"是复数形式，但汉语中"故事"没有复数形式，只有增加表示复数的词语"许多"，方可把汉语中的复数表达出来。

6. 出于汉语修辞的需要

翻译中的修辞性增词主要是解决词类转换后的表达问题，使拆离出来的部分在结构上更加完整，使译文合乎汉语表达习惯。

(1) As usual, happy families also had their own troubles.

【译文】 通常情况，幸福家庭也有幸福家庭的烦恼。

【评析】 句子中的"their own"译为"幸福家庭的"，修饰"troubles"，属于修辞性增词。

(2) One can't think of Africa without thinking of Egypt, the cradle of an ancient civilization, nor of Egypt without the Nile.

【译文】 想起非洲，人们不可能不想到作为古代文明发祥地之一的埃及。而想起埃及，也不可能不想到尼罗河。

【评析】 "nor of Egypt without the Nile"是"One can't think of Egypt without thinking of the Nile"的倒装省略结构。汉译时，应将省略部分补足，如上述译文，使结构对仗，意义完整。

（3）This thesis falls into introduction, literature review, study design and conclusion.

【译文】 这篇论文由前言、文献综述、研究设计和结论四部分组成。

【评析】 译文增加的概括词"四部分"使译文严谨、准确。

Versions for Appreciation（译文赏析）

（1）The past years have seen Baidu become not just one of the world's most popular Internet search engine, even a household word and a cultural phenomenon.

【译文】 过去几年里，百度不仅变成了世界上最受欢迎的搜索引擎之一，变成了一个家喻户晓的词语，甚至变成了一种文化现象。

【评析】 原文中动词"become"后面连跟三个名词充当其宾语，行文紧凑。但依此形式翻译，汉语译文将会句法松散，语义含糊，无法达到有效翻译的目的。译文三次重复"变成了"，句子层次分明，意义清楚，行文流畅。

（2）Hook your computer to the Internet and you are on your information superhighway.

【译文】 您只需把自己的电脑与互联网联通，便可以在信息高速公路上驰骋。

【评析】 如果将"you are on your information superhighway"译为"便可以在信息高速公路上了"，则显得晦涩、不流畅。增加辅助性动词"驰骋"后，句意完整，自然流畅。

（3）Investors and the public want more information on the economic, social and environmental impacts of organizations.

【译文】 投资者和公众希望更多地了解各位在经济、社会，以及环境等方面发挥的影响。

【评析】 句子中并列的几个同类词在译文中要增加"等方面"作为概括词，使译文更加符合汉语表达习惯。

（4）In accordance with the newspaper, the driver, who was returning from a wedding, seemed puzzled, "I only had two bottles of beer and a cocktail."

【译文】 据报道，那位参加完婚礼正在往回赶的司机一脸迷惑地说："我只不过喝了两瓶啤酒和一杯鸡尾酒罢了。"

【评析】 译文增加了语气词"……罢了"，淋漓尽致地将司机不负责任的态度刻画出来，准确展现原文意思。

（5）Vast flats of green grass, dull hued spaces of mesquite and cactus, little groups of frame houses, woods of light and tender trees, all were sweeping into the east.

【译文】 一片片茫茫的绿色草原，一簇簇色泽晦暗的牧豆树和仙人掌，一群群小巧的木屋，一丛丛轻枝嫩叶的树林——一切都向东奔驰。

【评析】 译文增加了叠字"一片片""一簇簇""一群群"和"一丛丛"，呼应了原文的复数概念，汉语叠字的魅力即刻展现出来，让读者产生听觉美感，享受到视觉美感。

（6）Predictably, this winter will be snowy, sleety and slushy.

【译文】 可以预言，今年冬天将雪花飘飘，雪雨交加，雪路泥泞。

【评析】 原文中三个"s"开头的词语，译文对应三个"雪"，既考虑到了汉语修辞的需要，又与原文有异曲同工之美，堪称成功之笔。

Questions for Teacher's Lecture（讲解题）

Translate the following sentences into Chinese.

（1）We don't give up; we never have and never will.

（2）Studies serve for delight, for ornament and for ability.

（3）Loss has been caused, terrible one.

（4）He just listened for a while and poohed her idea.

（5）Don't make such a fuss. It's nothing but a trifle.

（6）He described it—its forests, its little villages, its people, their fierce nationalism—with an eloquence that could arise only out of deep love for one's motherland.

（7） Mainly, we will conduct reform in the fiscal policy, the banking system, and state-owned enterprises.

（8） I believe this initial cooperation will lead more in the future.

Exercises for Students（练习题）

Translate the following sentences into Chinese.

（1） ——"Have you ever considered the influence your words have on the others?" the boss asked.

——"Never," he said.

（2） The BEC exam focuses on listening, speaking, reading and writing, especially on spoken English and practical business vocabulary.

（3） You are a real business negotiator.

（4） In fact it couldn't be easier.

（5） Her eyes were filling tears.

4.2　Omission in Translation（减词翻译）

英汉两种语言之间存在各种差异，有些词在英语中是必不可少的，而在汉语中却是多余的，翻译时，应该省略这样的词。减词并不意味着随意删除原文中的某些内容，而是出于译文语法、修辞或习惯表达上的需要。减词应遵循此原则：省略在译文中不言而喻，译出来反而生硬拖沓的词；省略不能有损原意或改变原文感情色彩。

1. 省略冠词

冠词是英语中有而汉语中无的词类。一般来说，除了带明显指示意义的定冠词和含有明显的"一个"或"每一个"意思的不定冠词要译出之外，其他冠词往往可省略不译。

（1） An administrator manager should make a plan for his organization.

【译文】　行政主管应该为组织制定计划。

【评析】　句子中的两个不定冠词"an""a"在此表示类别，在译文中可省略不译，使译文更加精练。

（2）Any home appliance must be handled with care whether it is a TV set, a VCR or a microwave oven.

【译文】　家电都需要轻拿轻放，不论是电视机、录像机还是微波炉。

【评析】　"a TV set，a VCR or a microwave oven"中的三个不定冠词"a"均为泛指含义，汉译时不必译出。

（3）The prosperity for our country's economy is bright.

【译文】　我国经济前景是光明的。

【评析】　专有名词前的定冠词"the"汉译时往往省略不译。

（4）Extra care should be taken to the old, the weak, the sick and the disabled.

【译文】　老、弱、病、残者应当给予特别照顾。

【评析】　原句中"the old, the weak, the sick and the disabled"均属"定冠词the＋形容词"的用法，表示一类或一群体人，这是英语中特有的用法，汉译时定冠词"the"省略不译。

2. 省略人称代词、物主代词和反身代词

汉语中较少使用代词，在意义足够明确的情况下，汉语中的代词可以省略。英译汉时，常常省略英语中做主语和宾语的人称代词，以及充当主语且表示泛指的人称代词。汉语中没有反身代词，翻译时一般省略英语中的这类词。

（1）He who has never reached the Great Wall is not a true man.

【译文】　不到长城非好汉。

【评析】　原句中"he"属于泛指概念，英译汉时省略不译。

（2）Manufacturer would also be required to disclose the hazardous contents of the products they buy and their plan for disposing of them.

【译文】　制造商还被要求公布其外购零部件所含的有害成分以及处理方案。

【评析】　省略原文中的物主代词"their"以及人称代词"them"。

如果将其译出来反而使译文累赘。

（3）We assure you of our prompt attention to this matter.

【译文】 我方保证立即处理此事。

【评析】 译文中省略物主代词"our"和人称代词"you"，这样不但不会影响读者对原义的理解，仅而使行文利落、干脆。

（4）They say forgive is divine. It may be good for your health, too, researchers report.

【译文】 常言道，宽容乃圣德。研究表明，宽容有益健康。

【评析】 为了简明、通顺起见，本句除了省略人称代词"they"之外，形容词性物主代词"your"也一并省略。

（5）Why do we feel cooler when we fan ourselves?

【译文】 我们扇扇子时，为什么会感到凉快些？

【评析】 本句省略了反身代词"ourself"。汉语中不存在反身代词这一类词，英译汉时无法对应，故省略。

（6）Mr. Brown glanced at his watch: it was 10:10.

【译文】 布朗先生看了一下手表，十点十分了。

【评析】 句子中省略了一个物主代词"his"和一个非人称代词"it"，使译文更加顺畅。

3. 省略连词

英语句子各个成分间多用连词来连接并构成相互关系，结构严密紧凑，以形显义。汉语句子各个成分间的关系多靠语义的贯通和语境的映衬，比较少用连接成分，其上下逻辑关系常常是暗含的，句间关系看似松散，实则以意统形。英译汉时，常常省略连词。

（1）We entered the railway station after crossing the road. While I was at the booking station buying a ticket, my classmate saw to my luggage.

【译文】 我们过了马路，进了车站。我买票，我的同学忙着照看行李。

【评析】 原句中的两个连接词"after"和"while"在译文中都被省略了。省略这些成分后，不但没有影响读者对原文的理解，译文反而更加言简意赅。

（2）Whatever you like to eat, just tell me.

【译文】 想吃什么，尽管告诉我。

【评析】 本句省略了连词"Whatever"。在不妨碍理解的基础上，可以省略连接成分。

（3）It may be a long time before an immigrant can fully get used to the customs and habits of the country to which he moves.

【译文】 要过很长一段时间，移民才能完全适应所移居国的风俗习惯。

【评析】 本句省略了连接词"before"，并对语序进行了调整。如将原文直译成"移民能够完全适应所移居国的风俗习惯之前需要很长一段时间"，会显得啰嗦，行文不畅。

（4）Even if you go there it won't do any good.

【译文】 去了也白去的。

【评析】 译文省略了"even if"。这是一个表示条件关系的主从复合句，根据汉语的语法特点，汉译时通常省略表示逻辑关系的连接词，语言扼要，句意清楚。

（5）We can not trust him, because comrade Li is not honest.

【译文】 李同志不老实，我们都不信任他。

【评析】 本句省略了连接词"because"。原句靠"because"将主句和从句整合为一体。汉语中，即使没有这样显性的衔接手段，句意仍然连贯、流畅。

4. 省略介词

英语句子中词与词、词组与词组之间的关系经常通过介词表示，常用的介词有 in、on、of、about、for、off、into、to、beyond、over、up、down、under 等。汉语则不然，各成分之间的关系往往依靠词序和逻辑关系体现出来，英译汉时，原文中的介词可省略不译。

（1）Smoking in public places is seriously prohibited.

【译文】 公共场所严禁吸烟。

【评析】 本句省略了介词"in"。表示地点的英语介词，译成汉语，往往省略不译。

（2）The ocean covers three quarters of the earth's surface, produces about 80 percent of all its life supporting oxygen, and is the driving force behind the entire weather system.

【译文】 海洋覆盖地球表面的四分之三。地球上维持生命的氧气约 80％产生于海洋，整个天气系统变化的动力也是海洋。

【评析】 介词"behind"省略不译。如直译成"整个天气系统变化背后的动力"显然不符合汉语的行文方式，省去介词后，反而简明、达意。

（3）At the age of 38, Mr. Wang was a university professor.

【译文】 王先生 38 岁就是一名大学教授了。

【评析】 原句中的介词"at"汉译时省略，译文简练、通顺。

5. 省略 it

英语中 it 作为代词，在句子中可用作主语、宾语、形式主语或形式宾语。it 的用法多样，除了用在强调句中外，还可以表示时间、地点、距离、气候等。但多数情形下，it 只起到语法上的作用，其本身并没有实际意义。英译汉时通常省略不译。具体情形如下。

1）充当形式主语或形式宾语时，it 常省略

（1）Later, he found it really hard to finish the problem on how the money supply affects the business cycle.

【译文】 后来，他发现完成对货币供应如何影响商业周期的研究的确很难。

【评析】 句子中的"it"用作形式宾语，译文中直接译出真正的宾语"完成对……的研究"，省略 it。

（2）It is very important that we seek sustained world peace and persistent global economic prosperity.

【译文】 非常重要的是，我们谋求持久的世界和平和全球经济发展。

【评析】 "it"在本句中是形式主语，真正的主语（逻辑主语）是"that we seek sustained world peace and persistent global economic prosperity"。由于真正的主语过长，为了保持句子结构平衡，通常借用"it"做形式上的主语，因为它无实际意思，不必翻译。

（3）It is not just small businesses that are developing a social and environmental approach.

【译文】 业务经营中注重社会效益和环保效益的并不只是些小型企业。

【评析】 "it"在句子中作为形式主语，无具体意义，可省去不译。

（4）Most experts think it easy to obtain sufficient electricity from these sources.

【译文】 大多数专家认为，从这些资源中获得充足的电力很容易。

【评析】 "it"在原句中做形式宾语，同样是出于平衡句子结构的需要，其真正的宾语是"to obtain sufficient electricity from these sources"。it 无意义，省略不译。

（5）We must not take it for granted that he is serving the people heart and soul.

【译文】 我们绝不可想当然地认为他是在全心全意地为人民服务。

【评析】 此句中的"it"为形式宾语，真正的宾语是"that he is ... heart and soul"，由于宾语较长故使用"it"做形式宾语，其本身没有实际意义，汉译时不必译出。

2）在强调句中省略 it

英语句子中常常用 it 充当形式主语，起到结构连接和平衡句子结构的作用，其没有真正的意义。常用的句型：It is + *n./ pron./* phrase + that-clause。

（1）It is from the sun that we get light and heat.

【译文】 正是从太阳那里我们得到了光和热。

【评析】 这是一个强调句型，强调的是介词短语"from the sun"。"It"在句子中没有实际的意义，只是引导出一个强调句。

（2）It is the old who know the history of the city.

【译文】 只有老人才会了解这个城市的历史。

【评析】 "it"在句中只起到引导强调句型的作用，其本身并无实际的含义，不必译出。

（3）It was not until the end of this year that our village has realized getting out of poverty.

【译文】 到了今年年底我们村才实现了脱贫。

【评析】 "It was not until...that"是强调句型，旨在突出脱贫的时间，将其译为"直到……才"，起到了同样的强调作用。

3）表示时间、距离、环境和自然现象时，省略it

（1）It was nearly getting dark when these pupils came back home from their school.

【译文】 这些学生放学回家时，天色几乎都黑了。

【评析】 "it"在此句中表示时间，译文中可省略，也符合汉语意思。

（2）It is very cold this winter.

【译文】 今年冬天特别寒冷。

【评析】 "it"在这里表示天气，汉译时省略。

（3）It was now the season for planting and sowing; many gardens and allotments of the villagers had already received their spring tillage.

【译文】 已是栽树和播种的季节，许多村民的园子和租种的耕地都已经耕种过了。

【评析】 "it"在本句中表示时间，但"栽树和播种的季节"已将时间的概念蕴含其中，故省略不译。

（4）Whatever you do and say, ask yourself whatever it is in the interest of the people.

【译文】 想想自己的一言一行是否符合人民的利益。

【评析】 汉译时可省略"it"，使整个句子简洁流畅。

6. 省略同义词或近义词

为了使句子的结构平衡，起到押韵的效果，达到强调的目的，英语中有时并用意义相同或相近的两个词。为了避免译文累赘晦涩，这时必须采用减词法。

（1）The undersigned sellers and buyers have agreed to close the following transactions according to the terms and conditions stipulated below.

【译文】 兹经买卖双方同意成交下列商品，特签订条款如下。

【评析】 条约、合同用语以精炼、简明为原则。本句中"terms and conditions"属同义词，翻译时需省去其中一个，否则译文啰嗦、拗口。

（2）Advertisements and commercials do many important things for society: they convey business information, facilitate communication and help keep the business world moving.

【译文】 广告对社会起了许多重要作用：传递商品信息，便于相互交流并促使商界正常运行。

【评析】 "advertisements"和"commercials"在汉语中的基本意思相同，为了避免重复翻译，只需翻出其中的一个，另一个省略不译。

7. 省略其他成分

英汉翻译时，往往省略某些成分，例如：反身代词、动词，或用缩译法、合并法等，使译文表达简洁、流畅。

1）省略同位语反身代词

When he was not engaging in business activities, Mr. Li himself worked intensively in his various laboratories.

【译文】 李先生不去从事商业活动时，就在不同的实验室中努力工作。

【评析】 原文中反身代词"himself"充当主语"Mr. Li"的同位语，以示对主语的强调，然而汉语中没有这一类的用法，翻译时省略。

2）从句缩译成一个简单句或一个词

The problem that we are considering is how to integrate the PC divisions in the two companies.

【译文】 我们正在考虑的问题是如何整合两家公司的个人电脑部。

【评析】 翻译此句时，将 that 引导的定语从句缩译成前置定语"正在考虑的"。

3）两个动词合并译

Intellectually, women want men to be equal parents and do their share.

【译文】 从理智上讲，女人希望男人也同样尽到养育孩子的职责。

【评析】 原句中"to be equal parents and do their share"为宾语补足语，意思是"做平等的父母，尽自己的责任"，汉译时将两个动词合并译成"也同样尽到养育的职责"。

4）有的动词不译出来

These developing countries cover vast territories, large population and abound natural resources.

【译文】 这些发展中国家土地辽阔，人口众多，资源丰富。

【评析】 译文省去了原文的谓语动词"cover"，行文紧凑。

Versions for Appreciation（译文赏析）

（1）The blooming flowers of the yard presenting a riot of color before my eyes quietly dispelled my grudges.

【译文】 就这样，面对这满院子灿烂的花，不说一句话，心中的怨恨已全消失了。

【评析】 原句中两个物主代词"my"在译文中省略不译。英语是形合的语言，讲究句子内部的排列和逻辑性。汉语是意合的语言，不拘泥于形式。因此，除非表示强调，物主代词通常不必译出，否则行文拖沓、生硬。

（2）The Nobel Prize started when Alfred Nobel wrote his last will and testament in 1895, leaving much of his wealth to the establishment of the Nobel Prize.

【译文】 1895年，阿尔弗雷德·诺贝尔订立最后的遗嘱，将其大部分财产用来建立诺贝尔奖，诺贝尔奖由此开始。

【评析】 本句省略了连接成分"when"。英语讲究形合，汉语注重意合，为了符合汉语的语法特点，通常省略原文中的连接词语。

（3）It is a fact that Americans and people around the world are sleeping less than they did just a decade ago.

【译文】 实际情况是，无论在美国还是世界其他国家，人们的睡眠时间比起10年前要少。

【评析】　本句的主语是"that Americans and people around the world are sleeping less than they did just a decade ago",由于主语过长,为使句子平衡,原句使用"it"做形式主语,以优化句子结构。汉语中没有对应的此类用法,故英译汉时将"it"省略。

(4) This has played a positive role and exerted a sound influence on enhanced cultural exchanges and friendship between the Chinese and British people and progress in science and technology as well as in thinking.

【译文】　这对加强中英人民的文化交流和友谊,推进科技和思想进步产生了积极的作用和影响。

【评析】　译文中省略了"positive"的同义词"sound",否则会使读者感到语义累赘。这两个形容词在本句中的意义相同,翻译时省略其中之一,译文简洁洗练。

(5) When the pressure gets low, the boiling point becomes low.

【译文】　气压低,沸点就低。

【评析】　本句省略了动词"gets"和"becomes"。如将此句翻译成"气压变低,沸点就变得低"会显得语句啰嗦,不符合汉语表达习惯。

Questions for Teacher's Lecture(讲解题)

Translate the following sentences into Chinese.

(1) But you don't have to eat anything to have an allergic reaction.

(2) Order is order; we cannot complain; we cannot bargain; we cannot question and we cannot suggest changes.

(3) She has distinguished herself in language talent.

(4) They claim that our environment is more important than our biologically based instincts in determining how we will act.

(5) It is indicated for the treatment of infection before the infecting organism has been identified or when caused by sensitive bacteria.

(6) I would like to make a brief statement regarding some of the

considerations leading to our affirmative vote.

（7）On July 4th, there are various celebrations throughout the United States.

（8）The products produced by this factory are good in quality and low in price.

（9）It is with this awareness that we came here to seek better ways to promote our cooperation.

（10）Neither party shall cancel the contract without sufficient cause or reason.

（11）The key to overcoming those challenges and the key to our success is constant innovation.

Exercises for Students（练习题）

Translate the following sentences into Chinese.

（1）The fear of being alone is a primary reason they are staying together.

（2）You are your greatest enemy if you are a coward, but if you are brave, you are your greatest friend.

（3）Before she could move, she heard a loud noise, which grew to a terrible roar.

（4）We have made much progress in pronunciation with the help of our teachers.

（5）It is good for health doing some exercises everyday.

（6）It is the uses to which television is put that determine its value to society.

（7）The Pacific alone covers an area larger than that of all the continents put together.

（8）A tariff may be defined as a tax which is put on a commodity when it crosses a national boundary.

4.3 Repetition in Translation（重复翻译）

在英译汉时，特定情况下需要重复已出现的词语，其目的是让译文的语义表达得更加清楚，更加生动，更有原文的精神和表现力，也更加符合中文的表达习惯。下面就一些常见的重复法予以归类、解释。

1. 语法性重复

汉语的重复不仅有韵律上的需要，还有语法上的需求。这里主要从重复名词和重复动词两个角度进行详细讲解。

1）重复名词

为了避免重复，英语表达有时较简练。但为了符合中文表达习惯，使句意明晰，英文原文中只出现一次的名词在译文中有时需要重复出现。

（1）Students should be cultivated to have the ability to analyze and solve problems.

【译文】 必须培养学生分析问题和解决问题的能力。

【评析】 "problem" 在原句中充当宾语，译文中重复翻译了"problem"，分别与"分析"和"解决"搭配，强调"问题"的重要性，读起来朗朗上口。

（2）In the following years, this technology has changed the method movies are made, shown and watched.

【译文】 接下来的几年，这项技术改变了人们制作电影、放映电影和观看电影的方式。

【评析】 译文中重复翻译了"movie"，并未增加多余信息，反而增加了译文的表现力，更贴近中文的表达习惯。

（3）The doctor will get more practice out of me than out of seventeen hundred ordinary patients.

【译文】 医生从我身上得到的实践，比从一千七百个病人身上得到的实践还多。

【评析】 译文重复了"实践",使句子意思通畅、完整。

(4) I knew every spot where a murder or robbery had been committed, or a ghost seen.

【译文】 什么地方发生过凶杀案或盗窃案,什么地方闹过鬼,我都知道。

【评析】 译文重复"什么地方",使句意表达得完整清晰,读起来有表现力。

(5) He became an oil baron—all by himself.

【译文】 他成了一个石油大王——一个白手起家的石油大王。

【评析】 译文重复翻译"石油大王",使全句通顺、完整。

2) 重复动词

中文中为了让句子意义明晰,有表现力和节奏感,有时会重复英文原文中的动词。

(1) We share one heart, one home and one glorious destiny.

【译文】 我们的心共同跳动,我们共住一个家园,我们也将共享一个荣耀的未来。

【评析】 译文三个动词分别为"共同""共住""共享",重复翻译了"共",使意思更加清楚,有表现力。

(2) Everyone wants great educational resources for their children, safe neighborhoods for their families and good jobs for themselves.

【译文】 每个人都想要他们的孩子获得优质的教育资源,想要他们的家人拥有安全的生活环境,想要他们自己都有好的工作。

【评析】 这里重复了"想要"。如果按照原句句式翻译,表达显得生硬。重复翻译"想要"使句意表达得更完整、顺畅。

(4) And time and again, it is to us that the people of this community have turned to get that balance right between the instincts to own your own house, your own home, to earn and spend your own money, to look after your own family.

【译文】 而且,社区的民众一次次求助于我们,以便在各种本能中求得平衡。这些本能包括拥有你自己的房子,拥有你自己的家,自己赚钱自己花,照顾你自己的家庭。

【评析】 该句汉译时在"your own home"前重复翻译了"拥有",使语义更加清楚,中文表达更有表现力。

(5) We are once again going to believe in ourselves and what we can achieve.

【译文】 我们要再次相信自己,相信我们能成功。

【评析】 重复翻译动词"相信"使译文通顺、完整。

2. 重复修饰语

为了忠实原文的精神或增加原文的表现力,有时在翻译修饰语时也需要重复。这里主要从重复形容词和重复做修饰语的副词两个方面进行解释。

1) 重复形容词

英译汉时,当原文中一个形容词修饰两个或多个名词时,根据具体情况,也可采用重译法,让译文句意清楚,表达顺畅。

(1) New records and invention are being made continually.

【译文】 新纪录和新发明不断产生。

【评析】 重复翻译"新"使语义更加清楚。

(2) Avoid using this computer in extreme cold, heat, dust or humidity.

【译文】 不要在过冷、过热、灰尘过重、湿度过大的环境中使用此电脑。

【评析】 这里重译"extreme",分别译为"过冷""过热""灰尘过重"和"湿度过大",使译文意思明确,表达顺畅、自然。

(3) They are loyal to the motherland and the people.

【译文】 他们忠于祖国,忠于人民。

【评析】 译文中的四字表达具有节奏感和表现力,重译了形容词"loyal"。

2) 重复做修饰语的副词

英译时,当原文中一个副词修饰两个或两个以上的形容词时,也可以重复翻译该副词,使句子更有表现力。

(1) Poetry is simply the most beautiful, impressive, and widely

effective mode of saying things, and hence its importance.

【译文】 诗歌只不过是最美丽、最感人、最有力的说话方式，这也就是诗歌的价值。

【评析】 副词"most"分别修饰"beautiful"和"impressive"，这里重复翻译为"最"。为了让译文保持节奏和表现力，"widely"也译为"最"。

（2）When her eyes looked up, they were very large, beautiful and attractive.

【译文】 她抬起眼的时候，眼睛显得很大，很美，很动人。

【评析】 "very"修饰三个形容词"large""beautiful"和"attractive"，分别译为"很大""很美"和"很动人"，体现出句中人物的美丽。

（3）It seems that these two branches of science are mutually dependent and interacting.

【译文】 似乎这两个科学分支是互相依存，互相影响的。

【评析】 "mutually"分别修饰"dependent"和"interacting"，译文中重复"互相"，形成两个四字表达，具有表现力。

（4）She is not aggressive or withdrawn.

【译文】 她为人从不咄咄逼人，也不畏畏缩缩。

【评析】 重复"不"使译文通顺、完整。

3. 重复代词所代替的名词

英文表达中有较多的代词，常交替使用避免重复。但是中文喜欢重复表达，明确句意。这里将从重复不定代词、重复物主代词、重复关系代词和重复人称代词四个方面进行详细解释。

1）重复不定代词

英文句子的衔接性往往通过代词体现，但是中文中使用代词的情况不多。所以，在翻译不定代词时，需要明确不定代词的意义，重复翻译不定代词所指代的具体内容。

（1）The room is warmer than the one downstairs.

【译文】 这间屋子比楼下那间屋子还要暖和。

【评析】 英语原句中为了避免重复，使用代词"one"替代了"room"。

但在中文中，要说清楚代词所指代的具体物体，因此将"one"译为"屋子"，恰如其分地再现原文的意思。

（2）A warrior knows another.

【译文】 英雄识英雄。

【评析】 译文重复翻译了"英雄"，明确"another"所指代的内容，符合中文表达习惯。

（3）Other substances, apart from organic ones, burn in air or oxygen.

【译文】 除有机物质外，其他物质在空气或氧气中也都会燃烧。

【评析】 重复翻译不定代词"物质"，明确"ones"指代的对象，句意明确。

（4）If you need any more money, you must get some out of the bank; there is hardly any in the house.

【译文】 如果你还需要钱，就得去银行取一些，家里没有多少钱了。

【评析】 原文"any"表达简洁明了，但汉译时，需要明确具体所指对象，这样更加符合中文表达，因此重复"钱"。

2）重复物主代词

英语中，物主代词分为形容词性物主代词和名词性物主代词。翻译这类代词时，为了让译文句意清楚且有表现力，在有些情况下也需要重复翻译。

（1）He is my love and soul mate.

【译文】 他是我的爱人，我的灵魂伴侣。

【评析】 译文重复了"我的"，强调"他"与"我"之间的关系，这样意义表达得更加清晰，译文也有表现力。

（2）This is our position, not theirs.

【译文】 这是我们的立场，不是他们的立场。

【评析】 译文重复了"立场"，明确了"theirs"具体所指对象，句意完整，符合中文的表达。

（3）A happy family also has its own troubles.

【译文】 幸福家庭也有幸福家庭的烦恼。

【评析】 重复翻译"幸福家庭"使句意完整。

3）重复关系代词

关系代词代表先行词，同时在从句中充当一定的成分。在翻译这类代词时，视具体情况，可使用重复译法，明确关系代词的具体意义。

（1）He who laughs last laughs best.

【译文】 谁笑到最后，谁笑得最好。

【评析】 译文重复"谁"，使表达的指向明确，意思完整，并起到增强语气的效果。

（2）The cat killed the rat that ate the malt that lay in the house that Jack built.

【译文】 杰克建了仓房，仓房里放着麦芽，麦芽让老鼠吃了，老鼠让猫杀死了。

【评析】 译文重复了"仓房""麦芽""老鼠"，并按照中文表达习惯调整了语序，句意清晰，表达顺畅。

（3）All these factors can be expressed as complex mathematical equations that can be solved by a computer to give the optimum route.

【译文】 所有这些因素都可以表示为复杂的数学方程式，这些方程式可用计算机计算，来得出最佳路径。

【评析】 译文重复了关系代词所指代的"方程式"，使句意更加明确。

（4）Context provides us with what Shinanoff call a "prescription that indicates what behavior is obligated, preferred, or prohibited".

【译文】 语境为我们提供了希纳诺夫所说的一种规定，这一"规定显示何种行为是强制的，何种行为更可取，何种行为要受到禁止"。

【评析】 译文重译了"that"所指代的先行词的具体内容"规定"，且句子从该处断开，符合中文的表达习惯。

（5）Practically all the theoretical deductions are substantiated by experimented data, much of which has been obtained in the author's laboratory.

【译文】 事实上，所有的理论推断均由实验数据证实，其中许多数据从作者的实验室中获得。

【评析】 译文重复了"数据"，明确"which"所指代内容，句意清晰。

4）重复人称代词

人称代词是代词的一种，用来直接指代某个（些）人或某个（些）物。在翻译人称代词时，同样需要视具体语境，采用相应的翻译方法，如重译法。

（1）Ocean does not so much divide the world as unite it.

【译文】 与其说陆以洋分，不如说是陆以洋合。

【评析】 重复翻译"陆"，并以四字词语体现，贴近中文表达。

（2）Men differ from brutes in that they can think and speak.

【译文】 人和兽类的区别，就在于人有思维而且会说话。

【评析】 译文重复翻译"人"，明确"they"所指代的内容，句意完整。

（3）How well the predictions will be validated by later performance depends upon the amount, reliability, and appropriateness of the information used and on the skill and wisdom with which it is interpreted.

【译文】 这些预测在多大程度上为后来的表现所证实，取决于所采用信息的数量、可靠性和适宜性，以及解释这些信息所用的技能和才智。

【评析】 译文重复了代词"it"所指的具体内容——"信息"，句意清晰，表达流畅。

（4）Reading makes us full, wise, progressive.

【译文】 读书使我们充实，使我们聪明，使我们进步，

【评析】 译文将原文中的"makes us"重复翻译，使语势有所加强，起到一种修辞效果。

Versions for Appreciation（译文赏析）

（1）Money is a good servant but a bad master.

【译文】 要做金钱的主人，莫做金钱的奴隶。

【评析】 重复名词"金钱"使译文明晰、具体，易于读者准确理解原

第 4 章 Translation Techniques of English Words Ⅲ（英语词语翻译技巧Ⅲ）

句的意义。

（2）Diplomacy was both an offensive and a defensive weapon. This was especially so because the city-states hired their soldier as contract labor.

【译文】 外交既是进攻性武器，也是防御性武器，在各城邦雇佣军队时尤其如此。

【评析】 译文重复"武器"，句意完整，自然流畅。

（3）And he knew how ashamed he would have been if she had known his mother and the kind of place in which he was born, and the kind of people among whom he was born.

【译文】 他知道，如果她知道他的母亲是谁，知道他出生在一个什么样的地方，知道他出生在什么样的人中间，他会感到多么羞耻。

【评析】 英文句子较难，译文若要将原句意思表达清楚，需要重复动词"知道"。

（4）The characteristics of his family claim some attention from all who would understand Napoleon and the influence which he was to wield over modern Europe.

【译文】 要了解拿破仑，了解他对现代欧洲的影响，就要对其家族特征予以一定的关注。

【评析】 重复动词"了解"使意义明晰、具体，易于读者准确领会原作者的意图。

（5）He hated failure; he had conquered it all his life, risen above it, despised it in others.

【译文】 他讨厌失败，他一生中曾战胜失败，超越失败，并且藐视别人的失败。

【评析】 译文明确"it"指代的内容，重复翻译"失败"，使得中文译文句意明确，且具有表现力和节奏感。

（6）A fog is similar to a cloud, except that it is formed on the ground rather than a thousand more feet up in the air.

【译文】 雾和云是相同的，只不过雾在地面上而不是在一千多英尺的高空形成的。

【评析】 译文重复"雾",明确"it"指代的内容,表达自然流畅。

Questions for Teacher's Lecture(讲解题)

Translate the following sentences into Chinese.

(1) The purposes of her journey were both military and political.

(2) Water can be decomposed by energy, a current of electricity.

(3) We must ensure that globalization benefits not only the powerful but also the men, women and children whose lives are ravaged by poverty.

(4) And I want to thank all of you, all of you here today and obviously everybody in the Conservative Party, for your hard work, for your campaigning, for your public spirit, and obviously for the extraordinary honor and privilege you have just conferred on me.

(5) He supplied his works not only with biographies, but with portraits of their supposed authors.

(6) He is a good student and son.

(7) People use natural science to understand and change nature.

(8) Sometimes clouds are dark simply because they are very thick.

(9) He is in need of an assistant for his research work, but he has not got a competent one.

Exercises for Students(练习题)

Translate the following sentences into Chinese.

(1) The purpose of radar is to obtain, process and display information.

(2) They would be very reluctant to postpone or cancel the meeting.

(3) Is he a friend or an enemy?

(4) On this day, we gather because we have chosen hope over fear, unity of purpose over conflict and discord.

(5) I have never been abroad, nor have I ever wished to go.

第 5 章

English Syntax and Translation
（英语句法与翻译）

5.1 Brief Introduction（简述）

贾玉新在《跨文化交际学》中将英汉语言在句法上的差异很精练地概括如下："英语高度形式化、逻辑化，句法结构严谨完备，并以动词为核心，重分析、轻意合；而汉语则不注重形式，句法结构不必完备，动词的作用没有英语中那么突出，重意合、轻分析。"句法的差异源于英汉思维的差异，是人们使用语言的不同习惯引起的。具体而言，句法现象主要体现在句子结构、语序、句子内容的表现手法等方面。英汉这两种语言在被动句、倒装句、简单句以及复合句等句子结构使用上差别很大，并且英汉复合句中的主句和从句之间在时间顺序、逻辑顺序等方面也有很大的差异，其先后顺序也不同。理解英汉句法各自的特点以及它们的异同，可以更好地帮助译者在处理两种语言时准确把握信息，恰当展现源语的特色和风格。

5.2 Differences between English and Chinese and Translation（英汉句子的差异与译法）

在翻译过程中，译者必须要研究、理解、掌握英汉句子间的差异性，恰当地呈现译文信息。要特别注意如下几个方面：英语重形合（hypotactic），汉语重意合（parataxis）；英语时态清晰，汉语时态隐含；英语句子重心在前，汉语句子重心在后；英语多用被动式，汉语多用主动式等。

1. 英语重形合，汉语重意合

英语重形合，句法结构严谨，表词达意强调准确。汉语重意合，句法结构松散。另外，英语语言表达直白，汉语表达的意思蕴藏在字里行间。英译汉时，应避免将英语重形合的特点迁移至重意合的汉语中，使得译文有太多的英语句法结构，所以，译者要尽力做到忠实于原文，但也要体现出汉语语言特征。

（1）This government of the people, by the people, for the people shall not perish from the earth.

【译文】 这个民有、民治、民享的政府是不会从地球上消失的。

【评析】 在此句中，英语注重以形显意，句子各成分之间的逻辑关系靠关联词等显性连接手段来直接表示，而译文没有形态变化的标志。英语中的关系词、连接词、介词、复合句都是采用了英语形合法的方式。翻译时需尊重不同语言的句法特点，避免"翻译腔"。

（2）With the development of economy and the coming of the information era, on the one hand, the Engel Coefficient reflecting the people's living standards has become lower and lower, which means the decrease in the food consumption but the increased expenditure in education and the information products.

【译文】 随着经济的发展和信息时代的到来，一方面，反应居民生活水平的恩格尔系数（表示人们的平均消费中，食品消费占总消费的比重）越来越低，这表明食物消费正在降低，教育和信息产品的消费增强。

【评析】 本句的译文基本上是按照原文的句法形式的顺序翻译的，即采用了形合法的形式。

2. 英语时态清晰，汉语时态隐含

时态是动词的形式与它所描述的动作或状态发生的事件之间的关系，属于语法概念。但是，汉语的动词形式不同于汉语，英语可以通过屈折变化来表示时间概念，而汉语语法的表现形式较隐匿。

在英语语法中，时间概念体现有三种方式：①词汇手段；②语法手段（即时态）；③序列手段（即语序）。作为一个语法概念，时态是具有屈折变化的综合型语言的一个典型特征。汉语是分析型语言，没有屈折变化，因此语言表达形式上看，汉语语法中没有时态标志，只能依靠词汇和语序手段，用语言表述体现时态，即先发生的先说，后发生的后说，而时间的转折跳跃则通常用词汇手段来体现。将既有综合型特征又有分析型特征的英语译为分析型语言的汉语，是一个不小的挑战。例如：

（1）Although we had followed this dire quest with every scrap of information imparted to us, we had not been told beforehand, or at any rate I did not know, the date of the decisive trial.

【译文】 虽然我们靠着他们提供的点滴情报，得以了解这项可怕研究的进展，但是关于这个决定性的试验日期，我们事先没有得到任何信息，不管怎样我是一无所知。

【评析】 本句译文经过了结构上的调整。在翻译过程中，译者没有拘泥于原文中语言结构的顺序。原文里用了两个不同的时态，同指一件事，前面用了过去完成时，后面用了一般过去时，但表意不同。"I did not know"是指当时讲话的情况。"we had not been told beforehand"是指事前没有人告诉这个消息。

可见，英语用语法现象来表明具体的时态概念，而汉语只能用表述方式来体现具体的时态概念。

（2）In one hour, Duke entered the orbit. And although there was too much to do to spend much time sightseeing, he did remember looking out the window a couple of times within the first hours.

【译文】 一个小时后，杜克进入了轨道。尽管要做的事很多，顾不上花很多时间欣赏外面的景色，他还是没有忘记在航程的头几个小时内曾几次向窗外观望。

【评析】 原文里时态清晰，用过去时态，原文用了"entered" "was"。而译文里时态模糊，没有明确地表示出时态概念。

（3）I had intended to call on you yesterday, but someone came to see me just when I was about to leave.

【译文】 我本来昨天要去看你的，但是刚要出门就有人来访。

【评析】 句中的"had intended"这个动作发生在"came"和"was about to"之前，也就是"过去的过去"发生的，所以用了过去完成时把时间先后清楚地表达出来。但是在汉语译文中，时间概念很模糊。

3. 英语句子重心在前，汉语句子重心在后

汉语句子重心一般落在句尾，语言表达层层铺设，交代完目的、条件、假设等次要内容后，再说出主要信息。英语则往往是句子重心（如判断、结论等）在前，次要的叙事部分（如描写、条件、假设等）在后。翻译时需要注意重心的转移。

（1）I am delighted to have the opportunity to speak this evening at the Sydney Institute on trade policy agenda.

【译文】 今晚上有机会在悉尼研究所就贸易政策的行动纲领问题做演讲，我感到非常高兴。

【评析】 本例原文句子重心应在"am delighted"上。不定式短语不是信息焦点，置于句末，遵循了英语句法中末端重量的原则，避免头重足轻。译文按照汉语先具体再评价的构句特点把"非常高兴"放到句尾。

（2）It was cruel to shut me up alone without a candle.

【译文】 把我一个儿关在里面，连支蜡烛也不点，真狠心呀！

【评析】 本例原文句子重心应在"cruel"上，不定式短语不是信息焦点，置于句末是为了平衡句子，遵循了末端重量的原则，避免头重足轻。译文按照汉语先具体再评价的构句特点把"真狠心"放到句尾表示感叹。

（3）The community services are more obvious for Tianhe District with a large number of highly cultivated people.

【译文】 对于拥有大量较高文化素质居民的天河区来说，社区服务现象尤其明显。

【评析】 英语中把句子重心"The community...obvious"放在句首，而汉语却把句子重心"社区服务现象尤其明显"放在句末。

4. 英语多用被动式，汉语多用主动式

英汉两种语言都有被动语态，但由于表达习惯上的差异，两种语言对被动语态的运用却不尽相同。同一个意思，英语往往使用被动语态来表达，而汉语则用主动语态来表达。例如："This novel was already written."（这本小说已经写好了。）。英语语法的严谨性使得句子必须有

主语，而汉语则不然，我们经常看到没有主语的汉语句子。英语绝大多数的及物动词和相当于及物动词的短语都有被动式。而汉语的被动意义常常用无主句、主语省略句、主语泛称句及其他句式来表示。尤其是在科技文体、新闻文体、公文文体及论述文体中，英语中常使用被动式。

（1）Science is discovered by a process of inquiry, observation, and experiment.

【译文】 科学的道理是通过询问、观察、实验这样一个过程发现的。

【评析】 被动意义在汉语中有时无需通过标志性的被动词语来体现。除了"被"字外，"让""给""叫""挨""受""遭""蒙""为"等也能构成被动语态。此句原文为被动语态，而译文译成主动语态。

（2）The environmental protection has to be recognized and attached importance（to）.

【译文】 人们必须去认识和重视环保问题。

【评析】 英语的被动式翻译成汉语时可使用通称做主语，如人、别人、某人、有人、人们、人家、大家等，保持汉语句子的主动性。

（3）The boss was much looked up to for his kindness.

【译文】 这个老板因多行善事而受人尊敬。

【评析】 原文使用了被动态"was looked up to"，而汉语译文中用了主动语态。

Versions for Appreciation（译文赏析）

（1）As water can float a ship, so can it swallow the ship.

【译文】 水能载舟，亦能覆舟。

【评析】 此句虽然是按照原文的顺序翻译，但译文还是以汉语表达习惯为准。

（2）They didn't give him a raise, though he had licked his boss's boots for years.

【译文】 尽管他这几年一直拍他老板的马屁，但他们并没有给他涨工资。

【评析】 根据英语表达习惯，较重要的信息一般置于句子前部，**翻译时把这个信息依照汉语的行文方式放到了后面。**

（3）Our International Club was founded a year ago to help foreign business in this city meet together.

【译文】 我们这个国际俱乐部是一年前成立的，目的是便于本城的外商聚会。

【评析】 原文用了被动语态"was founded"，但译成汉语时转换为主动态。

（4）To respond to the situation, we cooperate with the real estate companies, property management companies and professional IT enterprises to build the "web community" and make an e-living style possible for the residents, so that handling the office work at home, online shopping, online entertainment, good information consumption environment and "lifetime teaching" through the net-work are feasible.

【译文】 对此情况，我们的应对举措包括：联合房地产公司、物业管理公司和专业IT公司共同推进"网络社区"建设，创造数字家居生活，实现居家办公、网上购物、在线娱乐，提供良好的信息消费环境，帮助居民利用网络实现"终生教育"。

【评析】 原文中使用了三个不同的动词"cooperate""make""are"表述一般现在时的时态概念。而译文没有用文字直接表述时态概念。可以看出，英语时态清晰，汉语时态隐匿。

Questions for Teacher's Lecture（讲解题）

Translate the following sentences into Chinese.

（1）It is a wise man that never makes mistakes.

（2）I am very proud to have been brought up in a small town with a great sense of hospitality and voluntary service.

（3）The procedure is performed under local anesthesia in an outpatient facility.

（4）It is essential that every child have the same educational opportunities.

（5）Most of the questions have been settled satisfactorily; only the question of currency in L/C remains to be considered.

（6）Had you not helped us, we couldn't have finished the work.

（7）The key university is located near Zhongshan Park.

（8）Development of general key and support technologies that can promote structural upgrading will be accelerated.

Exercises for Students（练习题）

Translate the following sentences into Chinese.

（1）He had a disconcerting habit of expressing contradictory ideas in rapid succession.

（2）The many colors of a rainbow range from red on the outside to violet on the inside.

（3）It had been a fine, golden autumn, a lovely farewell to those who would lose their youth, and some of them lose their lives, before the leaves turned again in a peacetime fall.

（4）Television is the transmission and reception of images of moving objects by radio waves.

（5）We have already set up a special fund in the publicity and protection of the intellectual property rights, and also have established contingency planning mechanisms and provided financial aids to to enterprises in their overseas protection of rights, patent applications and research and development technological standards.

5.3　Translation on Negative Meaning in English Sentences （英语句子否定意义的译法）

英语经常使用词汇 no、not、none、never、neither、nor，以及含有否定意义的前后缀 in-、im-、no-、non-、un-、ab-、dis-、-less 等来

表示否定。而汉语最常使用的否定词就是不，以及毋、无、非、莫、没、别、甭等。另外，还可以使用一些特定的句法结构，如 too...to, prefer...to, prefer...rather than, know better than..., would...rather than 等。例如：

（1）It comes to nothing.（这事没有结果。）

（2）All that glitters is not gold.（闪光的未必都是金子。）

（3）He is a failure as an artist.（他是一个不成功的艺术家。）

（4）John is no poet.（约翰根本不是诗人。）

（5）It is a piece of wet paper.（这是一张未干的纸。）

（6）I don't know it.（我不知道这件事。）

1. 英语全否定与部分否定

英语常用表示"绝无"含义的单词表示全否定。汉译时一般只需把表示否定的不、无、非等词与动词连用，构成谓语的否定，即可表示全部否定和部分否定，例如：无、不、非、不全是、不都是、并非都、未必都等。

1）英语全否定的句子

表示全否定的含义时，常用 no、not、none、nobody、nothing、nowhere、neither...nor、never 等。

（1）The old man spent two hours in the supermarket, but he bought nothing.

【译文】 那位老人在超市待了两个小时，但他什么也没买。

【评析】 句中的"nothing"是全部否定的意思，表示"什么也没"。

（2）Never have we Chinese been daunted by any difficulties.

【译文】 我们中国人任何时候都没有被困难吓倒过。

【评析】 句子中的"never"是表示全否定的副词，置于句首更具有强调的语气。

（3）None of the answers are right.

【译文】 所有的答案都不正确。

【评析】 此句中的"none"是否定词，否定句中"answers"的正确性。译文为全否定。

（4）I don't know any of his work.

【译文】 我全然不知他的工作情况。

【评析】 此句中的"not...any"也是一种否定搭配的用法，表示全否定的意思。

2）英语部分否定的句子

表示部分否定时，英文常用 all、both、every、everybody、every day、everyone、many、everything、altogether、absolutely、wholly、completely、everywhere、always、often、entirely 等代词或副词与 not 连用。

（1）I don't know everything about the boy's study.

【译文】 这个男孩的学习情况我并不完全了解。

【评析】 此句中的"not...everything"表示部分否定的意思。

（2）All of what he says are not right.

【译文】 他所说的情况并非都是正确的。

【评析】 此句中的"all...not"表示部分否定的意思。

（3）We do not know all of these teachers.

【译文】 这些老师我们并非个个都认识。

【评析】 此句中的"not...all"表示部分否定的意思。

（4）Everyone can not answer this question.

【译文】 并非每个人都能回答这个问题。

【评析】 句中的"everyone...can not"表示部分否定。

（5）She is not entirely mistaken.

【译文】 她并没有完全弄错。

【评析】 句子中的"not + entirely"表示部分否定。

3）英语的否定前缀与后缀

英语词汇中的前缀和后缀也可以表示否定意思，例如 un-、in-、im-、ir-、-less 等。翻译时，常将这类词汇转化成汉语的否定句。

（1）The present international situation is unfavourable to that country.

【译文】 当前国际形势对那个国家不利。

【评析】 此句中的"unfavourable"表示否定的意思，译为"不利的"。

（2）It is impossible for him to accomplish the hard work in such a short time.

【译文】 要他在这么短的时间内完成这个艰巨的工作是不可能的事。

【评析】 句中虽无 not 等词，但"impossible"中前缀"im-"是表示否定的。所以，译文译成否定含义。

（3）The man is much irresponsible for what he has said.

【译文】 这个人对自己说过的话不负责任。

【评析】 句中的"irresponsible"意思是"不承担责任的、不可靠的"，此词中的前缀"ir-"表示否定。

（4）He remained speechless, with downcast eyes and flushing cheeks.

【译文】 他双眼朝下，两颊发红，仍然缄默不语。

【评析】 英语中 -less 是最常见的表否定的后缀。译文用"缄默不语"来体现原文的否定意思。处理这类合成词时需理解原文的否定意义，灵活处理成合适的汉语。

2. 英语双重否定

双重否定是指在同一个句子里出现两个否定词，即否定之否定。双重否定句表示的意思是肯定的。译成汉语时一般同样译成双重否定式，但有时也可译成肯定式。

（1）There is not any advantage without disadvantage.

【译文】 有一利必有一弊。

【评析】 汉语译文采用肯定式处理，英语用了双重否定"not"和"without"，但译文根据原文语境灵活选用汉语句式，采用肯定式，真实再现原文语气。

（2）We must never stop taking an optimistic view of life.

【译文】 我们对生活要永远保持乐观的态度。

【评析】 汉语译文采用肯定式处理再现原文语气。

（3）It is not impossible to master a foreign language within a short period of time if you use a good study method.

【译文】 如果你学习方法对头，那么在短时间内掌握一门外语并不是不可能。

【评析】 原文中的"not"和"impossible"在一起表示双重否定，译成"不是不可能"，译成两个否定，即肯定的意思。也可译成"是可能的"。

3. 英语宾语从句的否定

英语具有否定转移功能。当英语句子主句中的谓语是 fancy、confirm、know、guest、prove、believe、consider、expect、fear、hope、imagine、suppose、think、trust、guess、figure、reckon、find（感到）、anticipate 等表判断心理活动的动词时，否定词 not 通常置于该动词前面，逻辑上却否定从句的内容，即否定含义从主语的谓语转移到宾语从句的谓语。也有一些情况下不发生否定转移，例如：当 think、expect 用作"料想"时以及 suppose、think 用于祈使句式或被副词修饰时，上述动词与情态动词一起构成否定。

（1）He does not consider that she is a novelist.

【译文】 他认为她不是一个小说家。

【评析】 根据欧美人的思维习惯，not 逻辑上是否定后面宾语从句的，所以译成汉语时要真实体现原文实际意思。

（2）I didn't think the paper had been written by him.

【译文】 我认为这篇论文不是他写的。

【评析】 从句中出现否定转移，转到宾语从句上。形式上"not"否定"think"一词，但实际上是否定了宾语从句的谓语动词。

（3）I wouldn't say that the book is worth reading.

【译文】 我认为这本书不值得一读。

【评析】 句子中的"wouldn't say"从形式上看是否定"say"，但实际上，否定词 not 已经转移，否定宾语从句的谓语动词。

4. 英语无否定形式的否定

某些英文句子结构形式上是肯定的，而意思是否定的。对于结构形式上肯定但意义否定的句子，我们不可拘泥于原文的结构，翻译时，应将原文译成汉语否定意思。

（1）The beauty of the park is more than words can describe.

【译文】 这公园的风景美得无法形容。

【评析】 此句中的"more than...can"从结构形式上是肯定的,其实,相当于"can not",意思是"简直不、无法、难以",译成汉语为否定形式。

(2) The younger teacher is short in teaching experience.

【译文】 这个年轻教师没有什么教学经验。

【评析】 句中的"short"从形式上看是肯定的,实际上是"短缺、不足",应译成否定意思。

(3) The truth turns to be quite other than what I think.

【译文】 事实真相与我想的完全不同。

【评析】 原文中的"other than what I think"形式上是肯定形式,但译文中为否定意义。

5. 英语几种表示否定意义的句型可以译成汉语肯定意思

英语中的否定意义还可以使用一些特定的句法结构来表示,例如:too...to,否定结构 + until, no one(nothing)...so...but...,否定结构 + neither(nor)+ be, fall short of..., prefer...to, prefer...rather than, know better than..., would...rather than 等。

(1) No man is so foolish but he may give another good advice sometimes.

【译文】 无论怎样愚笨的人有时都能够给别人好的忠告。

【评析】 这是一个否定意义的句型"no...so...but"。如果翻译成"没有什么人那么愚笨,但是他可以能够给别人好的忠告",则会让人不知所云。

(2) We must be never too old to learn.

【译文】 我们应该活到老,学到老。

【评析】 翻译英文的否定形式时应该根据汉语的语言习惯灵活处理,力求用恰当的汉语译文,切不可生搬硬套。

(3) No work is so difficult but we can accomplish it.

【译文】 没有什么工作是我们不能完成的。

【评析】 "no...so...but"是否定意义的句型。假如翻译成"没有什么工作那么难,但是我们能完成",则会让人不知所云。

Versions for Appreciation(译文赏析)

(1)Mr. Wang cannot thank me enough because I help him with his study.

【译文】 由于我帮助他学习,王先生对我感谢不尽。

【评析】 若译成"他不能足够地感谢我"会显得死板、拗口,不符合汉语语言习惯。

(2)We have very seldom seen such beautiful park.

【译文】 我们很少见到过如此美丽的公园。

【评析】 句中的"seldom"具有否定意义,意为"很少",译文为否定意义,符合汉语习惯。

(3)Vegetarians are known for their abstention from eating meat.

【译文】 众所周知,素食者不吃肉。

【评析】 单词"abstention"中前缀"ab-"含否定意思。

(4)The swimmers should know better than to go swimming right after eating.

【译文】 游泳者应该知道,饭后不能立即去游泳。

【评析】 原文具有隐含的否定意义,所以译文再现了原文的否定含义。

(5)We simply don't think he will give me a hand when we are in difficulty.

【译文】 我们根本不指望他在我困难的时候能帮助我们。

【评析】 原文中"simply don't think"为否定式,副词"simply"修饰"don't",否定形式不发生转移,即否定主句而非从句。

(6)No energy can be created , and none destroyed.

【译文】 能量不能创造,也不能消失。

【评析】 原文中的"no"否定主语"energy",译文中转换成否定谓语"be created",否定词"none"否定谓语"destroyed"。

(7) I don't suppose that they will object to my suggestion.

【译文】 我想他们是不会反对我的建议的。

【评析】 原文中"don't"实际上否定宾语从句的谓语"object"。

(8) Under no circumstances he would work hard.

【译文】 在任何环境下，他都不会努力工作。

【评析】 句中的介词短语"under no circumstances"是否定形式，否定句中的谓语"work"。

Questions for Teacher's Lecture（讲解题）

Translate the following sentences into Chinese.

(1) I do not remember all these new words.

(2) Nothing in the world is difficult for one who sets his mind to it.

(3) Actually, the most outstanding contributions made by Chinese nation to world civilization by no means limited to the Four Great Inventions.

(4) You can't make something out of nothing.

(5) He was not weak never to resume his work again.

(6) Qian Xuesen's contribution to modern science can scarcely be overrated.

(7) We didn't think he is such a selfish man.

(8) Now no spaceship cannot be loaded with man.

(9) He would rather die of hunger than steal.

(10) Your temper is more than I can bear.

Exercises for Students（练习题）

Translate the following sentences into Chinese.

(1) Since we are no sages at all, who may avoid making mistakes?

(2) Not everybody can enjoy this piece of music.

（3）All the foreigners cannot pass the borders without visas.

（4）The student did not sit in the classroom listening to the teacher.

（5）Instead of attempting to save one species at a time, they are trying to save a complete natural environment.

（6）Nothing daunted, the hero dived into the icy water for rescuing a child from drowning.

（7）Science has no enemy but the ignorant.

（8）He would hardly recognize his hometown if he saw its changes now.

（9）Her explanations were met with blank incomprehension.

（10）His failure was due to nothing else than his own carelessness in the examination.

（11）The traveller entertained his host with stories, some of which were really more than could be believed.

5.4　Translation of Attributive Clauses and Adverbial Clauses （定语从句和状语从句的翻译）

英语定语从句分为限制性定语从句和非限制性定语从句，一般放在被修饰词后，其差别在于限制意义的强弱。而汉语中的定语一般放在修饰词前面。在翻译时，一定要考虑汉语表达的习惯。若英语定语从句过长，就不宜译成汉语中的定语。

英语中引导状语从句的连词在汉语中几乎都可以找到对应的词。但是，翻译起来也并非易事。由于两种语言的表达方式不同，英语句子多用连词，而汉语用得比较少。因此在翻译中要采用灵活多样的方法，来处理复杂结构的问题。

1. 英语定语从句的翻译

英语的定语从句有限制性和非限制性的，常见的引导词有who、which、that、when、where、as等。要善于从原文的字里行间发现信息逻辑上的关系，然后译成汉语中相应的偏正复句，还可使用带"的"

字的定语词组、后置并列分句、独立句等。

1）限制性定语从句的翻译

较短的限制性定语从句可以在翻译时将其置于先行词前。

（1）This is a photograph I took during my trip to Russia.

【译文】 这是一张我去俄罗斯旅行时拍摄的照片。

【评析】 "I took...to Russa"是一个限制性的定语从句，把整个从句译成"……的"，直接放在先行词"照片"的前面。

（2）Space and oceans are the new world which scientists are trying to explore.

【译文】 太空和海洋是科学家们努力探索的新领域。

【评析】 译文把定语从句"which scientists...to explore"译成陈述词组，直接置于先行词前面，修饰先行词。

（3）He is not a young man whom I admire.

【译文】 他不是我敬佩的年轻人。

【评析】 译文将原文的定语从句"whom I admire"译成陈述词组，置于先行词前面做定语，修饰先行词。

2）非限制性定语从句的翻译

非限制性的定语从句一般比较长，最常见的翻译方法是与主语分开，单独译成一个句子。例如：

（1）We took a short cut through the woods, which saved about 10 minutes.

【译文】 我们抄近路穿过树林，这样我们少花了 10 分钟。

【评析】 "which saved about 10 minutes"为非限制性定语从句，可单独译成一个句子。

（2）John is a wise young man, who works hard at study.

【译文】 约翰是一个聪明的年轻人，他学习很刻苦。

【评析】 原文的"who works hard at study"为非限制性的定语从句。在翻译时单独译成一个句子，用来解释主句。

（3）The man, who you despise so much, is a very useful talent.

【译文】 虽然你非常瞧不起那个人，但他是一个很有用的人才。

【评析】 可将非限制性定语从句"who...so much"译成一个让步状语从句，修饰整个主句。

2.英语状语从句的翻译

英语中引导状语从句的连词在汉语中大多可以找到对应的词，例如：because、since、when、while、if、though 等。英语状语多用连词，而汉语多依靠语句中的词序和语序来表达相关意思。所以，要注意状语从句的多种译法。

（1）I have a right to criticise you because I am your advisor.

【译文】 我有权批评你，因为我是你的导师。

【评析】 此句由连词"because"引导一个原因状语从句。连词"because"在汉语中可直接译为"因为"。

（2）Why did you tell lies when you know the truth?

【译文】 既然知道事实真相，为什么要说谎呢？

【评析】 将"when you know the truth"译为让步的分句，符合汉语表达习惯。

（3）The rain is not likely to stop for some time，so we had better hurry.

【译文】 这场雨一时不可能停下来，我们还是赶快走为好 。

【评析】 句中的"so we...hurry"由连词"so"引导一个结果状语从句。译文中虽未译出"所以"，但也包含了因果关系。

（4）Our scientists have been working hard to advance artificial intelligence so that computers can do even more work for human beings.

【译文】 我国科学家们一直在努力工作以加速发展人工智能的步伐，让计算机为人类做更多的事情。

【评析】 原文"so that...human beings"为目的状语，说明科学家们这样做的目的。译文准确表达了原文的意思。

Versions for Appreciation（译文赏析）

（1）It is also an opportunity to open up the Chinese car industry for modern technology and for the creation of new jobs and more prosperity.

【译文】 这对于开放中国汽车工业、发展现代技术、创造就业机会、实现进一步繁荣，也是一个机会。

【评析】 此句是一个简单句。原文中的"It"是形式主语，"to open up... more prosperity"是真正的主语（逻辑主语）。翻译时必须调整句子结构，把动词不定式译成主语，这样显得流畅，也符合汉语表意。

（2）The official circulation of euro on January 1st of this year marks a new step toward the European integration from which businesses from every part of the world including those from China will benefit a lot such as cost cut.

【译文】 今年1月1日欧元正式流通标志着欧洲一体化进程又迈出了新的一步，包括中国企业在内的各国企业都将得到交易成本降低等益处。

【评析】 原句中的"from which businesses from every...from China"是介词＋关系代词引导的限制性定语从句。由于原文句子很长，将定语从句拆开，单独译成一个句子，译文就很清楚。

（3）I should have been afraid to touch a horse when alone, but when he told to do it I was disposed to obey.

【译文】 我要是只有一个人是不敢去碰一匹马的，但既然他吩咐我去干，我也就乐意服从了。

【评析】 此句中的两个时间状语从句分别转译为表示假设的分句和表原因的分句。如果把"when"译成"当……时候"，就会过于死板，言不达意。

Questions for Teacher's Lecture（讲解题）

Translate the following sentences into Chinese.

（1）Even in the European Union investment in traffic infrastructure is mainly driven by public investment.

（2）More grain will be produced this year than last year.

（3）He who respects others is constantly respected.

（4）How happy we are when our friends are coming from afar.

（5）He gave up literary study when he might have made a great career in it.

（6）Nothing has happened since we parted.

（7）Those who are in favor please hold up their hands.

（8）Unfortunately, many countries in the world have trade barriers which are designed to protect their economy against international market forces.

（9）The tram stopped, which caused me to come late.

Exercises for Students（练习题）

Translate the following sentences into Chinese.

（1）It is not long ago that energy markets within the European Union were deregulated and liberalized.

（2）So far the experience with private providers indicates, that energy can be offered very efficiently on a private basis.

（3）There is no denying that the new method has greatly raised labor productivity.

（4）The lake, which forms the eastern boundary of our farm, has always played an important part in our lives.

（5）As is known to all, 2003 saw the successful launching of China's first manned spaceship.

（6）We tramped through the city for over one hour until we arrived at the high speed railway station.

（7）They become desperate for work, any work, which will help them to keep alive their family.

（8）Since the reform and opening-up, the logistics industry has made great achievements in its reform and development and has stimulated the rapid development of national economy.

5.5 Translation of Similar English Sentences（英语相似句子的译法）

从结构形式看上，英语有些句子很相似，有的只是一词之差，或标点符号不同，但意义却大相径庭。所以在翻译实践中需要仔细区分这些句子的意思，才能将其含义准确地表达出来。比较下列句子：

（1）A. I have a friend, who is a teacher.

B. I have a friend who is a teacher.

【译文】 A. 我有个朋友，他是个教师。

B. 我有个当教师的朋友。

【评析】 A 句中的 who 引导非限制性定语从句，含有"我可能只有一个朋友是当教师的"的意思。B 句中的 who 引导限制性定语从句，含有"我可能不止一个朋友，可能有两个、三个或更多"的意思。所以，要尽可能翻出原文所表达的隐含意思。

（2）A. I feel that I have nothing to write.

B. I feel that I have nothing to write with.

【译文】 A. 我觉得我没有什么可写的。

B. 我觉得我没有写字的东西。

【评析】 A 句指没有可写的内容或事情，所以应翻译成"没有什么可写的"。B 句指没有用以写字的钢笔、铅笔之类的工具，所以应翻译成"没有写字的东西"。要注意这两句话的区别。

（3）A. His son is an only child.

B. His son is only a child.

C. Only his son is a child.

【译文】 A. 他的儿子是个独苗。

B. 他的儿子只不过是个孩子。

C. 只有他的儿子是个孩子。

【评析】 A 句中的 only 是形容词，意思是"唯一的"，所表达的含义是他的儿子是独生子女，所以将"an only child"译成"独苗"。B句中的only是副词（只不过），所以"only a child"译成"只不过是个孩子"。C句中的only也是副词（只有，仅仅），表明了其他人都是成人，只有他一个人是孩子，所以C句译成"只有他是个孩子"。

Versions for Appreciation（译文赏析）

（1）A. How beautiful is the painting?

B. How beautiful is the painting!

【译文】 A. 这张画有多好看？

B. 这张画多好看啊！

【评析】 "how"可当疑问副词或感叹词。A句是由"how beautiful!"引起的特殊疑问句，翻译成相对应的疑问句"这张画有多好看？"。B句是由"how"构成的感叹句，译成感叹句"这张画多好看啊！"。

（2）A. You should not work too hard.

B. You can't work too hard.

【译文】 A. 你不应该太拼命。

B. 你再怎么努力也不为过。

【评析】 A句的"should not"是否定"study too hard"的，意思为"太努力不好"，所以"should not study too hard"译成"不应该太拼命"。B句中的"can't"虽然也是否定"study too hard"，但意思是"不可能会努力过度"，应译成"再怎么努力也不为过"。两者的意思不同。

（3）A. The professor had a word with John.

B. The professor had words with John.

【译文】 A. 教授跟约翰交谈了一下。

B. 教授跟约翰吵了一架。

【评析】 "have a word with sb."意思为"talk with sb."，译为"交谈"。而"have words with sb."意思为"quarrel with sb."，应译为"吵架"。

Questions for Teacher's Lecture（讲解题）

Translate the following sentences into Chinese.

（1）A. Here comes the bus!

B. The bus comes here.

（2）A. Mr. Wang went to bed about ten yesterday evening.

B. Mr. Wang went to sleep about ten yesterday evening.

（3）A. One girl can finish that work.

B. A girl can finish that work.

（4）A. Mary was with child.

B. Mary was with a child.

（5）A. She admired me as he.

B. She admired me as much as him.

Exercises for Students（练习题）

Translate the following sentences into Chinese.

（1）A. Mr. Zhang came here before long.

B. Mr. Zhang came here long before.

（2）A. Master Li has repaired his car.

B. Master Li has his car repaired.

（3）A. The organization must look to the incident.

B. The organization must look into the incident.

（4）A. All of us saw a great many men there.

B. All of us saw many a great men there.

5.6　Translation of Special English Sentences（英语特殊句型的翻译）

英语中特殊句型的结构比较固定，能够从中发现一些普遍性的规律，如何运用好符合汉语习惯的表达方式，将英语特殊句子译成准确的汉语，这也是翻译中的一个重要问题。例如：

（1）Were it not for your help, I wouldn't have got what I have today.（要是没有你的帮助，我就不会有今天。）

（2）Many a time has his teacher given him serious criticism.（好多次他的老师都对他提出了严厉批评。）

（3）Now comes your turn.（现在该轮到你了。）（主谓倒装）

（4）He loves the girl. So does she him.（他爱这个女孩，这个女孩也爱他。）

（5）How happy the Chinese people are today!（今天中国人民是多么幸福啊！）

（6）A discussion is going on how to serve the people heart and soul.（关于如何全心全意为人民服务的讨论正在进行中。）

（7）The sun will never, it is true, rise from the west.（不错，太阳绝不会从西方升起。）

1. 英语倒装结构翻译

英语的倒装句是指一个或一个以上的句子成分由于自然语序中的位置被移动前置而形成的一种句式，主要是指逻辑主语出现在动词（谓语动词、助动词等）后，动词后面的成分出现在句首。句子倒装可能出于语法结构要求和修辞的需要。倒装结构可以起到突出成分和强调语义的双重效果。

（1）Here is the book you want.

【译文】 你要的书在这儿。

【评析】 "here"置于句首，谓语动词"is"放在主语"book"之前。

（2）On with your clothes!

【译文】 穿上你的衣服！

【评析】 "on"置于句首，使句子倒装，有强调的作用。

（3）Long live the solidarity of the people of the world!

【译文】 全世界人民大团结万岁！

【评析】 "long live"置于句首，这是表示祝愿的倒装句，有时可加上

"祝""祝福"等词,也可译成"祝愿全世界人民大团结万岁!"。

(4) Only in the industrious way can we learn English well.

【译文】 我们只有勤奋才能学好英语。

【评析】 "only + 状语"位于句首表示强调时采用倒装结构,这是为了修饰状语。

(5) Young as she is, she has made great contributions for our country.

【译文】 她虽然年轻,但为国家做出了重大贡献。

【评析】 "as"引导倒装结构,加强这个让步从句的语气。

(6) So fast did he walk that none of us was his equal.

【译文】 他走得如此之快,我们没有一个人赶得上他。

【评析】 "so...that"从句中,"so"居于句首引导倒装句,起到修辞效果。

2. 英语分隔结构翻译

在英语句子中,两个结构关系密切或意义紧密相连的成分应尽量紧挨在一起。但有时因为表达、修辞、句型等原因,需要在这些紧密相连的成分之间插入一些其他成分,从而造成了分隔现象。例如:

(1) Many years ago some people brought forth on this island, a small nation, and dedicated to the proposition that all men are created equal.

【译文】 很多年前,有一些人在这海岛上创建了一个小国家,并奉行人人生来平等的原则。

【评析】 "bring forth"(产生)和"a small nation"(一个小国家)之间被"on this island(这个小岛)分隔,"dedicated"修饰"a small nation"。因为"a small nation"的修饰语较长,所以将其后置。

(2) Abraham Lincoln is the most famous instance of the claim that Americans often made that in their country a man may rise from the lowest to the highest position.

【译文】 美国人常认为:在他们国家,一个人可以从社会最底层上升到社会的最上层,亚伯拉罕·林肯就是极好的例子。

【评析】 "the claim"和其同位语"that in their country a man may rise...the highest position"被"the claim"的定语从句"that Americans often made"分隔。对同位语从句的翻译采用顺译法,将同位语从句译成分句,也可使用冒号、破折号等。

(3) "No, no; it is, it is, it is his very own letter!"

【译文】 "不,不!这封信的的确确就是他本人亲笔写的!"

【评析】 该句话将原文出现了三遍的"it is"译为"的的确确",达到了突出、强调的效果。

3. 英语多枝共干结构翻译

多枝共干结构是英语中一种常见的结构,其特点是一个动词可以有两个或多个宾语,一个名词可以有两个或多个定语,两个或几个名词也可以有一个定语,两个或几个介词也可以有一个宾语等。这种结构使行文简洁,避免重复。在科技文献中,常见多枝共干结构,很容易引起理解或翻译的困难。翻译时,往往采用重复译法,要按汉语的习惯处理好词与词之间的搭配。

1)英语主谓搭配翻译

主语和谓语是句子中的主要成分。在大多数情况下,一个句子都有主语和谓语,而且要保持一致性。

(1) John sits on the grassland, props up his feet, smokes and stares into space.

【译文】 约翰坐在草地上,支着腿,抽着烟,凝视着空中。

【评析】 此句有一个主语和四个并列谓语动词。翻译时,采用顺译法,按照原文语序翻译。汉语句中使用一连串动作"坐在草地上""支着腿""抽着烟""凝视空中",生动地刻画出约翰的形象。

(2) Mary sees Jack and comes and sits at the same table.

【译文】 玛丽看见了杰克,就走了过来和杰克坐到一张桌子前。

【评析】 此句主语的三个并列谓语"sees""comes""sits"用"and"连接起来,表示三个动作发生的连续性。

2)英语动宾搭配翻译

所谓动宾搭配就是动词跟宾语搭配在一起。

(1) The old man experienced overwhelming fatigue, muscular stiffness and loss of appetite and weight.

【译文】 这位老人之前感到极度疲乏、肌肉僵直、食欲不振，体重也减轻了。

【评析】 原文中"fatigue"和"stiffness"和"loss"均为动词"experience"的宾语。

3）英语定心搭配翻译

在英语句子中，往往会出现一个名词被一个或几个定语所修饰，或被一个短语或几个短语所修饰，这个被修饰的词语被称为中心词。

（1）Intense light and heat in the open contrasted with the coolness of shaded avenues and the interior of buildings.

【译文】 露天场所的强烈光线和酷热，同林荫道上和建筑物内部的凉爽形成了对比。

【评析】 在该句中，"in the open"修饰"heat"和"light"。此外"intense"是"light"和"heat"的定语。句中的"coolness"既被后置介词短语"of shaded avenues"修饰，也被"the interior of buildings"修饰，只是"the interior of buildings"前省略了介词"of"。翻译时，搞清楚词与词之间的关系，再准确地译成汉语。

（2）They are school personnel largely composed of teachers, students and staff.

【译文】 他们都是学校成员，主要有教师、学生和职工。

【评析】 句中的"largely composed of teachers, students and staff"是分词短语做定语，修饰"personnel"。

4）英语系表搭配翻译

英语系表结构说明物质的一个性质，而不是一个动作，构成是主语＋系动词＋表语。系动词本身有一定的词义，但不能独立充当谓语，是起修饰作用的。系动词有 be、feel、sound、taste、seem、smell、turn、get、become、look 等。

（1）Do you think, because I am poor, obscure, plain, and little, I am soulless and heartless?

【译文】 难道就因为我一贫如洗、默默无闻、长相平庸、个子瘦小，就没有灵魂，没有心肠了？

【评析】 这是著名小说《简·爱》中的经典语句。第一个系动词"am"后有四个表语，第二个系动词"am"后有两个表语。作者使用这些简洁直接的词语，节奏感极强，很容易调动读者的情绪，引起共鸣。汉译时，将第二个"I am"省略，以达到简洁连贯的效果。

（2）Good medicine tastes bitter to the mouth.

【译文】 良药苦口。

【评析】 句子中的"tastes"为系动词，后面的"bitter to the mouth"是"tastes"的表语。

（3）I know, Lily is beautiful, cheerful and intelligent.

【译文】 我知道，莉莉面容姣好、性格开朗、头脑聪明。

【评析】 此句中，"is"（系动词）后，有三个形容词描述莉莉的特点，"beautiful"是形容容貌的，"cheerful"是形容性格的，"intelligent"是形容头脑的。译成中文时，将这些词增补进去，使意思更加明了。

（4）His accounts seemed to me to smell of truth.

【译文】 他的叙述在我看来似乎有点真实性。

【评析】 句子中的"seemed"为系动词，和后面的"to smell of truth"构成系表结构，为合成谓语。"to me"为状语。

5）英语动状搭配和介宾搭配翻译

英语中的很多副词和介词短语都可以当状语修饰动词，表明动作的状态。

（1）Professors always check essays and make experiments carefully and objectively to verify them.

【译文】 教授们总是检查论文的情况，并且细心而客观地做试验加以验证。

【评析】 句中的"carefully"和"objectively"共同修饰动词"make"。汉译时，只要译出一个"make"即可使译文简洁明了。

（2）We should use the application of the machines, products and systems of applied knowledge that scientists and technologists have created.

【译文】 我们应该运用机器、产品以及科学家和技术人员建立起来的应用知识体系。

【评析】 介词"of"后面有三个宾语:"machines""products""systems"。汉译时,"of"前面的名词"the application"可以不重复译出,译成"运用机器、产品以及体系",这样使语言简洁、连贯,而不是译成"运用机器、运用产品、运用体系"。

(3) This is occurring as global companies pursue regional solutions from a manufacturing and supply chain perspective.

【译文】 这种情形出现时正值全球企业力图通过制造业和供应链的渠道来解决地区性的问题。

【评析】 句子中的介词"from"和宾语"a manufacturing and supply chain perspective"搭配,构成"介词+宾语"结构,在句中当状语。

6)英语混合搭配翻译

英语句子的结构比较复杂,往往存在着词与词、短语与短语、从句与从句、主句与从句等之间混合搭配的关系,翻译时,要首先了解句子的结构。

(1) Talking helps kids build a vocabulary, and is building block of reading, forgetting the baby talk. However, if you use real words for objects and people, kids quickly learn the meaning of big words from the context.

【译文】 谈心帮助孩子们积累词汇,是给阅读打底子,不过别像婴儿学舌,要用真人真事的词语来说,你用大词儿,孩子们也会从上下文很快领会词义的。

【评析】 本句的主干是"Talking helps kids build a vocabulary",句中后面的叙述都是与主干混合搭配的部分。

(2) First aspect of science is the application of the machines, products and systems of applied knowledge that scientists and technologists develop.

【译文】 科学的第一个方面就是运用机器、产品和科学家、技术人员研制出来的应用知识体系。

【评析】 句子中的定语从句"that scientists...develop"修饰"systems of applied knowledge",而"of the machines, products, and systems of applied knowledge"充当定语修饰"application","of applied knowledge"充当定

语修饰"systems"。这是一个多层混合搭配修饰语的句子。

Versions for Appreciation（译文赏析）

（1）At that moment I heard a song to my side and turned my head. There stood a singer.

【译文】 正在那时，我听见旁边有歌声，扭头看去，那儿站着一名歌手。

【评析】 此句主语为"a singer"，谓语为"stood"，这是倒装结构，就正常语序为"a singer stood there"。翻译时可按照原文的语句顺序翻译，即"那儿站着一名歌手"，保留原文的修辞效果。

（2）And on the topmost spray of the tree there blossomed a marvelous rose, petal following petal, as song followed song.

【译文】 在树最高的枝头上开放出一朵不寻常的玫瑰，花瓣一片一片地开放了，歌儿也唱了一首又一首。

【评析】 英语原句中主语太长，故将状语提前，以保持句子平衡，同时强调状语"on the topmost spray of the tree"，以增强效果。汉译时，可保留原文的语序，将其句子成分一一译出。

（3）Nobody can be a great scientist who does not realize that as a scientist it is her first duty to follow her intellect to whatever conclusions it may lead.

【译文】 要成为一个科学家，首要的责任就是按照自己的理性思考去得出结论，不管得出什么结论。如果意识不到这一点，任何人就不可能成为伟大的科学家。

【评析】 修饰主句主语"nobody"的定语从句"who...it may lead"被句子的复合谓语分隔开。由于定语从句比较长，翻译时改变原句结构，重新组合。另外，还可将定语从句转译为条件状语从句。

（4）"They are never alone," said Sir Philip Sidney, "that are accompanied by noble thoughts."

【译文】 菲利普·希尼爵士说过："有高尚思想陪伴的人是永不孤

独的。"

【评析】 句子中修饰"They"的定语从句因为较长而后移，于是形成了谓语、状语、插入语对它们的分隔，避免了头重脚轻的问题。但在翻译成中文时，应将该插入语"said Sir Philip Sidney"放到句首，以符合中文的表达习惯。

（5）It is now strictly true that scarce a fly or mosquito can be seen in the town and cholera is no more.

【译文】 城里几乎看不见苍蝇和蚊子，霍乱也已经绝迹了，这是千真万确的。

【评析】 该句很容易误译成"城里几乎看不见苍蝇和蚊子，这是千真万确的，而霍乱也已经绝迹了。"其实，在"and"后面省略了从属连词"that"，句中"that scarce a fly or mosquito"和"(that) cholera is no more"两个并列主语从句共用同一谓语动词"is"。所以汉译时，应将"这是千真万确"这一形式主语从句译文放在句末，先译逻辑主语从句"城里几乎看不见苍蝇和蚊子"和"霍乱也已经绝迹了"，句末译出这两个事实是"千真万确的"。

（6）Scientists use these probes to eliminate the problems and errors associated with theoretical analysis.

【译文】 科学家们使用这些探测器解决了理论分析产生的问题，并消除了理论分析所产生的误差。

【评析】 宾语"problems"和"errors"共用一个谓语动词"eliminate"，应采用重复译法，并应注意动词和宾语的意思要搭配正确，应译成"解决问题"和"消除误差"这两个短语，使其合乎汉语的表达习惯。

（7）In several years the novelist has written many novels and excellent plays on social problems.

【译文】 几年里，这个小说家写了许多有关社会问题的小说和优秀剧本。

【评析】 两个名词"novels"和"plays"共用一个定语"on social problems"。翻译时，不必将"on social problems"重复译出，"有关社

会问题的小说和优秀剧本"这一短语意思明了。

（8）This system neither receives energy from, nor gives energy to, anybody outside it.

【译文】 这种系统既不从外界任何物体吸收能量，也不向外界任何物体释放能量。

【评析】 句中"receives energy from"和"gives energy to"共用一个宾语"anybody outside it"，在英译汉时，要将"anybody outside it"重复译出，即译成汉语"不从外界任何物体吸收能量，也不向外界任何物体释放能量"，使汉语句子行文流畅。

Questions for Teacher's Lecture（讲解题）

Translate the following sentences into Chinese.

（1）Scarcely any enemy planes were left undamaged after the People's Liberation Army of China attacked.

（2）Students with good study habits can obtain a lot more in their scholastic achievements than those without.

（3）I told my students in detail how these scientists overcome all the difficulties.

（4）China, in fact, has caught up with the world advanced levels in many ways.

（5）There will be times when, if you decide not to look up a reference, you will miss something that may be important.

（6）His diligence, earnestness, carefulness and brilliance, made him praised by all.

（7）Never will we give up the great experiment for the national construction.

（8）Whole our people are determined to build our motherland into a modern powerful socialist country.

（9）We have never seen such a face so sweet, happy and radiant.

（10）The Heavenly Lake, which is one of the world famous scenic spots, is on Tianshan Mountain.

（11）He differed from his colleagues in that he devoted his spare time to make the scientific research.

（12）You don't seem to know when you're lucky.

Exercises for Students（练习题）

Translate the following sentences into Chinese.

（1）Hardly had we gathered in the wheat when it began to rain.

（2）It is because it was worth doing rather than because it was profitable that I took over the job.

（3）We are very proud that the environments of our country are getting more and more beautiful.

（4）Then came the hour we had been looking forward to.

（5）Here came frightful days of snow and rain.

（6）Whether we work or sleep, are earnest or idle, rejoice or moan in agony, the river of time flows on with the same resistless flood.

（7）Of all these dreams the last is, I believe, the only legitimate one.

（8）They took it for granted that students love and respect their teachers.

（9）They had a long, hard, but interesting journey.

5.7 Translation of English Relative Clauses （英语关系分句的译法）

在关系代词that、which、who、whom、whose等和关系副词when、where等引导的定语从句中，先行词后面可由关系代词引导从句补充信息。而汉语由于缺乏关系代词、关系连词等连接手段，通常用时间或逻辑来表明句意。翻译时，若要将带有关系分句的英语翻译成语序正确的汉语，就要将英语关系分句译成前置定语，或者并列、独立的分句或简单句。翻译时可采用合译法、分译法和融合法。以下四个例句运用了三种译法。

（1）We witnessed that the prosperity which has never been seen before appears in the countryside.

【译文】 我们见证了农村出现了前所未见的繁荣。

【评析】 译文将定语从句前置。

（2）Our university boasts a big, well-equipped library which has earned enduring fame throughout the country.

【译文】 我们的大学拥有一个设备良好的大型图书馆，它在全国享有持久的声望。

【评析】 译成并列分句。

（3）Yuan Longping is an academician who has been making the greatest contribution for having studied the fine varieties of rice.

【译文】 袁隆平院士为水稻优良品种的研究做出了最重大的贡献。

【评析】 译文将定语从句前置。

（4）There is a teacher outside who wants to see you.

【译文】 门外有个老师要见你。

【评析】 译文将定语从句和主句的先行词融为一体。

1）英语关系分句合译法翻译

在翻译英语定语从句时，可把定语前置或前移，将英语关系分句译成汉语带"的"字的定语成分，这就把英语复合句译成了汉语单句。例如：

（1）I was, to borrow from John Le Carre, the spy who was to stay out in the cold.

【译文】 借用约翰·勒·卡雷的话来说，我成了一个被打入冷宫的间谍了。

【评析】 此句中的关系分句"who...in the cold"修饰先行词"the

spy"。搞清主从句的逻辑关系是译文准确恰当的前提。

（2）The people who worked for him lived in mortal fear of him.

【译文】 在他手下工作的人对他怕得要死。

【评析】 译文中将关系分句"who...in mortal"前移，符合汉语表达习惯。

（3）This is a top heavy social structure where an aging population outnumbers the younger generation.

【译文】 这是一个老年人多于年轻人的失衡的社会结构。

【评析】 "where"引导的定语从句修饰"structure"，将关系分句译为前置定语，修饰先行词"social structure"，符合中文的表达习惯。

2) 英语关系分句分译法翻译

当英语关系分句与其先行词或与其他句子成分关系较松散，且译成汉语前置定语显得太长时，可将关系分句译为并列分句或独立分句，要注意适时重复或省略先行词。有些关系分句中的隐藏逻辑关系可译为带有原因、目的、结果、条件等的偏正复句。例如：

（1）He unselfishly contributed his uncommon talents and indefatigable spirit to the struggle which today brings them within the reach of a majority of the human race.

【译文】 他把自己非凡的才智和不倦的精力无私地奉献给这种斗争，这种斗争今天已让人类中大多数人可以达到这些目标。

【评析】 当从句结构复杂，译成汉语前置定语从句显得太长，不符合汉语表达习惯时，可以译成后置的并列分句，并且重复先行词。

（2）They are striving for the ideal which is close to the heart of every Chinese and for which, in the past, many Chinese have laid down their lives.

【译文】 他们正在为实现一个理想而努力，这个理想是每个中国人所渴望的，在过去，许多中国人为了这个理想牺牲了自己的生命。

【评析】 原文从句很长，结构复杂，很难译成汉语前置定语从句，可以译成后置的并列分句。

（3）The dog that worried the cat that caught the rat that ate the grain.

【译文】 耗子把粮食吃光，猫把耗子抓伤，狗把猫逼上房。

【评析】 把关系分句译为并列分句，符合时间先后顺序，且先行词的重复使译文更地道。

（4）The plan is original and heroic, which pleased all of them.

【译文】 这方案新颖且有魄力，所以他们都喜欢。

【评析】 主句与关系分句之间实际上存在因果关系，这样翻译更符合汉语逻辑思维。

3）英语关系分句融合法翻译

融合法，又称简化法，就是把原句中充当主语的先行词与关系分句融合在一起译成一个独立句子，尤其适用于"there + be"结构中带有关系分句的句型。这样可把主句和分句合译成一个简单句，关系分句则译成简单句的谓语。例如：

（1）"We are a nation that must beg to stay alive", said a foreign economist.

【译文】 一个外国经济学家说道："我们这个国家不讨饭就活不下去"。

【评析】 此句译文把主句和关系分句融合成一个句子。若把关系分句和主句分开，译成"我们是一个不讨饭就活不下去的国家"，则不符合汉语表达习惯进行，显得死板拗口。

（2）There was another student who seemed to have answers.

【译文】 另外一名学生似乎有了答案。

【评析】 翻译时"there was"省略不译，关系分句译为"似乎有了答案"，采用了融合法。

Versions for Appreciation（译文赏析）

（1）The sun, which had hidden all day, now came out in all its splendor.

【译文】 那个整天躲在云层里的太阳，现在又光芒四射地露面了。

【评析】 此句的关系分句（即定语从句）直接译成定语，修饰主句的主语，主句的谓语部分单独译成一句。

（2）He liked his sister, who was warm and pleasant, but he did not liked his brother, who was aloof and arrogant.

【译文】 他喜欢热情友好的妹妹，而不喜欢冷漠高傲的哥哥。

【评析】 此句较长，可把分句简化成形容词，这样就能把主句从句合译为一个单独的句子。

（3）When we praise the Chinese leadership and the people，we are not merely being polite.

【译文】 我们对中国领导人和中国人民的赞扬不仅仅是出于礼貌。

【评析】 这是一个主从复合句，译者把"When we...the people"译成一个词组，从而使译文变成一个简单句。

（4）He would be a shortsighted commander who merely manned his fortress and did not look beyond.

【译文】 （谁如果）只守城堡而不往远处看，（那他）就是目光短浅的指挥官。

【评析】 此句采取分译法，把关系分句"who merely...look beyond"与主句分开。

（5）There is no predicting when there will be an earthquake here.

【译文】 这个地方何时发生地震无法预测。

【评析】 此句中的先行词"predicting"和关系分句"when there ...here"融合译成一个独立句子，"there is"省略不译。

（6）Key universities have many excellent teachers who can culture hundred of top talents.

【译文】 重点大学的优秀教师可以培养许许多多的顶尖人才。

【评析】 译文把关系分句"who can culture...talents"和主句融合在一起，译成一个句子，采用了融合法。

（7）World War II was, however, more complex than World War I , which was a collision among the imperialist powers over the spoils of markets, resources and territories.

【译文】 第一次世界大战是帝国主义列强之间争夺市场、资源和领土的冲突，而第二次世界大战比第一次更复杂。

【评析】 译文将关系从句"which was...and territories"与先行词"World War I"融合翻译成一个单独的分句,符合汉语句子的行文习惯。

Questions for Teacher's Lecture(讲解题)

Translate the following sentences into Chinese.

(1) He had talked to Vice President Nixon, who assured him that everything that could be done would be done.

(2) One was a violent thunderstorm, the worst I had ever seen, which obscured my objective.

(3) She likes the person, who is warm and pleasant.

(4) This is a very good film which is about the Chinese revolution.

(5) Several youngsters who had no home to go to were wandering in the street.

(6) The letter which he received yesterday announced his father's death.

(7) He is a professor who gives lectures in several universities this semester.

(8) There is an old lady who lives at the foot of the mountain.

(9) There has never been a man around me who likes going shopping.

(10) There are lots of people who want to travel in outer space.

Exercises for Students(练习题)

Translate the following sentences into Chinese.

(1) The men had suddenly awakened to the fact that there were beauty and significance in these trifles, which they had so long trodden carelessly beneath their feet.

(2) Oceans are the new world which scientists are trying to explore.

(3) They have fostered several children whose worlds have been

shattered during the battle.

（4）A young married couple interested me who were unlike any people I had ever known.

（5）Stratford is the place of Shakespeare which many have longed for.

（6）There are many people who like this film.

（7）The little girl knew the sequestered spots where the hens laid their eggs.

（8）After dinner, the four key negotiators resumed their talks, which continued well into the night.

（9）He saw in front that haggard white-haired old man, whose eyes flashed red with fury.

（10）He liked his sister, who was warm and pleasant, but he did not like his brother, who was aloof and arrogant.

5.8 Translation of Long and Difficult Sentences in English（英语长句和难句的译法）

英语中常用连词、介词、分词短语和由关系代词、关系副词引出的各种从句组成长句，有时甚至一整段只由一句话构成。处理长句时首先要从语法上分析全句，弄清长句中几层意思间的关系。只有先搞清句子结构，才能确定使用何种翻译方法和技巧。常用的翻译长句的方法有顺译法、逆译法、分译法、插入法和重组法。例如：

（1）With an awareness of history and current situation, we have gradually adopted a scientific development model, which aims at developing the economy refraining from resources lavishness, environment deterioration and social disharmony.

【译文】 历史文脉和现实感知，使我们逐步确立了科学的发展观，即坚持发展经济不以浪费资源、不以牺牲环境、不以破坏社会和谐为代价。

（2）Through education, we expect to create a human environment, in which knowledge is valued, innovation is appreciated and encouraged, and the right post is assumed by the right person, so that the sustainable development capacity and civilization in our country can be improved.

【译文】 我们期待通过教育，造就崇尚知识、激励创新、贤者在位、能者有职的人文环境，增强我国的可持续发展能力。

1. 顺译法

有些英语句子虽然长，但其逻辑关系、表达顺序与汉语表达基本一致，层次分明。处理时可按照原文的叙述顺序翻译成汉语。

（1）From the standpoint of the developing countries, the next decade should see a greatly accelerated program for scientific and technological cooperation aimed at widespread dissemination of technology for meeting the basic needs of man, such as nutrition, shelter, communication, health and sanitation.

【译文】 从发展中国家的角度来看，下一个十年应该有一个大力加速科技合作的计划，旨在广泛地传播技术，满足人们对营养、住宅、交通、卫生保健的基本需要。

【评析】 此句虽然很长，但是在翻译过程中基本没有将原文的叙述结构进行调整，仍然按照原文语言结构的顺序翻译，采用了顺译法。

（2）The parties, adhering to the principle of equality and mutually benefit and through friendly consultation, desire to exert all their efforts in cooperating with each other and agree to jointly invest to set up a joint venture enterprise in Nanjing, the People's Republic of China for the purpose of expanding international economic cooperation and technological exchange on a mutually beneficial and profitable basis.

【译文】 双方本着平等互利的原则，通过友好协商，愿尽全力相互合作，共同投资，在中华人民共和国南京市建立合资企业，在互惠互利的基础上，扩展国际经济合作和技术交流。

【评析】 本句虽长，但只有一个主语（parties）和两个谓语（desire 和 agree），两个谓语之后各接一个动词不定式短语充当宾语，主语后接一个分词短语充当后置定语，而且句子的主语又是分词的逻辑主语。结构分析之后，可以采取顺译法。

2. 逆译法

针对英语的长句表达次序与汉语表达习惯不同，甚至完全相反的情况，需要从原文的后面往前翻译，即采用逆译法进行翻译。

（1）It was not enough that each office there was an intelligence agent or informer like their typist.

【译文】 每个办公室都安插了一个像她们的新打字员那样的间谍或告密者，好像还不够似的。

【评析】 本句中的逻辑主语过长，从英语语言结构的角度出发，一般要用一个形式主语 it 放在句首，逻辑主语置于其后，这样可以平衡句子结构。翻译成汉语时，采取逆译法，将真正的主语先译。

（2）The United Nations is attempting to settle conflicts around the world that have taken a terrible toll and misused the earth's resources.

【译文】 世界上的各种冲突有的已造成可怕的后果，有的滥用了地球的资源。联合国正试图消除这种冲突。

【评析】 翻译时将句子中说明事实的部分，即造成后果的部分先译出来，采用了逆译法。

3. 分译法

分译法就是把长句翻译成几个简短的句子。也就是说，从句、分词、动名词、不定式短语、名词短语、形容词、副词等，都可以译成一个独立的汉语句子。例如：

（1）But on one final point Mr. Brown, who has a raspy voice and a sly smile and looks a bit Dick Cheney, wants to be clear.

【译文】 不过，在最后一点上，布朗先生打算说得十分明白，他嗓子嘶哑，面带狡诈的笑容，模样有点像迪克·切尼。

【评析】 译文把"who has a raspy voice and a sly smile and a bit Dick Cheney"拆成三个分句，译成三个汉语句子。这样，句子表达清晰，简单明了，也符合汉语表达习惯。

（2）It is right here, at Geneva, whose very name evokes peace, the will to peace, cooperation among nations, that after long years of discussion, the negotiations were completed which had started on March 24, 1984 at Havana on the necessity of creating as part of the United Nations system a body responsible for regulating international trade.

【译文】 日内瓦是一个唤起和平，唤起各国和平意愿与合作的地方。正是在此地，于1984年3月24日始于哈瓦那的旷日持久的谈判终于完成了。这次谈判的主题是是否有必要在联合国系统内建立一个负责调节国际贸易的机构。

【评析】 本句很长，但译者把它拆成五个分句翻译成汉语句子。翻译时，原句的叙述结构只是按照汉语表意的需要，做了一点调整，如："It is right here"调到中间和"that after long years of discussion...which had stared on... Havana"一起翻译成一个句子。本句还是采用了分译法。

4. 插入法

在英译汉中，有时使用破折号、括号或冒号，把句中难以处理的成分和解释性的成分插入其中。

（1）The second aspect is the application by all members of society from the government official to the ordinary, of the special methods of thought and action that scientists use in their work.

【译文】 第二个方面就是全体社会成员（从政府官员到普通公民）都使用科学家们在其工作中所采取的那种特殊的思考方法和行为方法。

【评析】 在翻译"all members of society"时，为了使译文表达更加清楚，用括号把解释性的词语括在其中。

（2）If you go to visit Nobel's old residence, the house in which the great chemist remained a bachelor throughout his life, you will catch sight of a shelf laden with experimental records.

【译文】 如果你参观诺贝尔的故居——在那座房子里，这位伟大的化学家过了一辈子独身生活——你会看到一个堆满实验记录的书架。

【评析】 对原句中定语从句的翻译，采用了插入破折号的做法，使译文自然流畅。

5. 重组法

翻译英语长句时，常常使用多种方法，解决翻译中遇到的各种疑难问题。重组法就是要打破原句语言结构的顺序，进行调整和组合。

（1）People were afraid to leave their houses, for although the police had been ordered to stand by in case of emergency, they were just as confused and helpless as anybody else.

【译文】 尽管警察已接到命令，要做好准备以应对紧急情况，但人们不敢出门，因为警察也和其他人一样不知所措，无能为力。

【评析】 本句中的"for"引导一个原因状语从句，其中又含有一个让步状语从句。如果译成"人们不敢出门，因为虽然警察已接到命令，要做好准备以应对紧急情况。但他们也和其他人一样不知所措"，就会显得生硬。按照汉语表达习惯将原句结构进行调整之后，译文就清晰、流畅多了。

（2）I was touched on the raw when the teacher criticized those pupils who often came to school late.

【译文】 当老师批评那些上课经常迟到的学生时，他触到了我的痛处。

【评析】 句子中的"when the teacher...to school late"时间状语从句里又含有一个定语从句。汉译时间状语从句时，把定语从句译成"pupils"的前置定语，然后把主语从句调整到最后翻译。

Versions for Appreciation（译文赏析）

（1）The cooperation is a natural step for both companies as they both share the same science-based culture as well as a common vision concerning the future of the industry.

【译文】 本次合作对两家公司而言，是很自然的。因为双方有相同的以科技为本的文化，并对本行业未来的发展有着相同的理念。

【评析】 本句虽长，但还是一个简单句。所以翻译时，不需要对原句的叙述顺序及其结构进行调整，直接采用顺译法翻译。

（2）I think if I were starting over, I'd try and do something on my own. I don't think I can stand here and say that I'd go for a big corporate life.

【译文】 我想，如果我可以从头开始，我会选择自己创业，我不会说我要进入大公司。

【评析】 在翻译此句时，可以按照原文叙述的顺序翻译，不需要进行语言结构调整，可采用顺译法。

（3）It is the shared wish of all the people and a common responsibility for all countries to build a better and prosperous world through cooperation and development and common winning.

【译文】 加强合作，促进发展，实现共赢，使我们的世界变得更加美好，是各国人民的共同愿望，也是国际社会的共同责任。

【评析】 根据汉语表达的需要，译者把介词短语"through cooperation and development and common winning"放到句首，然后把"It is the shared wish...for all countries"放到最后，采用了逆译法，使得译文更加自然、流畅，更加符合汉语表达习惯。

（4）It is necessary to facilitate multilateral and bilateral cooperation in trade and promote regional economic cooperation.

【译文】 应该加强多边和双边贸易合作，积极推进区域合作，这是有必要的。

【评析】 译者把"to facilitate multilateral and...regional economic cooperation"这个介词短语提到句首，而把"It is necessary"放到最后，采用了逆译法，符合汉语表达习惯。

（5）Within the global village, Asia has found itself in a unique position. This position is unique because the potential for growth in Asia is as great as our cultural heritage and diversity.

【译文】 在地球村中（这是一种比喻，指现代科技的发展，缩小了地球上的时空距离，国际交往日益频繁，整个地球就像茫茫宇宙中的一个小村落。）亚洲享有独特的位置。正如我们丰富的文化遗产和文化多样性一样，亚洲发展的潜力同样是巨大的。

【评析】 在翻译此句时，须将"the global village"的这个概念插入译文中进行注释，使读者更加了解"地球村"的基本意思。

（6）And while the preferential policies of some of these special zones will gradually disappear under the WTO, the complexities of doing business in such a vast market will not.

【译文】 尽管在中国加入 WTO 以后某些区域的优惠政策会逐渐取消，但在这样一个巨大的市场里开展业务的复杂性并不会消失。

【评析】 翻译此句时，必须将句子的叙述结构顺序做一些调整，如：把"under the WTO"调到"the preferential policies of some of these special zones"前面，将"in such a vast market"提到"complexities"前面，采用重组法。

Questions for Teacher's Lecture（讲解题）

Translate the following sentences into Chinese.

（1）I think each country will develop its economy in the way that suits its particular history, its particular culture and its own people.

（2）In terms of China itself, some executives of some companies still drool over the prospects of selling their goods or services to a single market of 1.4 billion people.

（3）It is the responsibility of the international community and requirement of sustained development of the world economy to help developing countries develop themselves and close the widening gap between the South and North.

（4）It is quite understandable that the United Nations, having no life except that which its members give to it, should show evidence of the maladies that is present in the world today.

（5）I must say that his statement was laudable for its frankness and quite plausible on the basis of premises which, I'm afraid, are invalid in the context of the United Nations Charter.

（6）It remains to be seen whether the reserves of raw materials would be sufficient to supply world economy which would have grown by 500 percent.

(7) As far as sight could reach, she feasted her eyes on a vastness of infinite charm, which presents itself in a profusion of color, in verdant luxuriance, in dulcet warbling, in pervading perfume, in rippling undulation, in cataract sprays, in hilly waves, in field crisscross and verily in vitality and variety.

Exercises for Students（练习题）

Translate the following sentences into English.

(1) The prospects for this year remain favorable, although growth is likely to be at a slower, more sustainable pace.

(2) It is quite obvious that the organization of such a computer becomes rather complex, since one must insure that a mix-up does not occur among all the various problems and that the correct information is available for the computer when it called for, but if not, the computation will wait until it is available.

(3) The reality is that anyone focused solely on the short-term gains or anyone who is prone to impatience is destined to be disappointed.

(4) A crimson blush came over Juliet's face, yet unseen by Romeo by reason of the night, when she reflected upon the discovery which she had made, yet not meaning to make it, of her love to Romeo.

(5) It is common experience that a certain amount of regular exercise improves the health and contributes to a feeling of well-being whether or not exercise adds to the length of life.

(6) This land, which once barred the way of weary travelers, now has become a land for winter and summer vacations, a land of magic and wonder.

第 6 章

Literal and Free Translation in English
（直译法与意译法）

直译和意译是翻译中两种最基本的表达方法，各有优缺点。直译就是在保持原文语言形式不变的基础上，用地道的译入语（target language）准确再现原作的内容和风格。意译则是舍形式而取内容，不拘泥于原文的句法手段、选词用字、修辞手段等。当代美国翻译家奈达有句名言："Translation means translating meaning.（翻译就是翻译意思。）"。可见，直译和意译，都要遵守一个根本的宗旨——翻译意思。

总的来说，直译反映语言之间的共通之处，意译解决语言之间的差异。最佳的翻译方法就是通过英、汉两种语言特点的对比，分析其异同。英语和汉语的结构有相同的一面，汉译时可直译，忠实原文内容。由于这两种语言之间还有许多差别，这时就需要意译。特别要注意的是，直译不等于死译，意译也不等于乱译。

6.1　Literal Translation（直译）

季羡林先生认为："所谓'直译'是指原文有的，不能删掉；原文没有的，不能增加，这与译文的流畅与否无关。"直译从内容到形式都贴近原文，可以保留原文的表达方式，既忠实又传神，是一种较为理想的表达方法。在译入语的语言条件许可的情况下，直译的译文应该既保留原文的内容、格调，又保留原文中的形象比喻、民族色彩、地方色彩等。请看下列短语翻译。

wash one's hands 洗手
army corps 军团
artificial selection 人为选择 / 人为淘汰
double digit growth 两位数增长
multinational corporation 跨国公司
directed credit 指导信贷
corruption-free environment 清廉的政府
preferential trade treatment 优惠贸易待遇
information age 信息时代

patent rights applications 专利申请
high-tech industry 高新技术产业
residential community 居民社区
property management 物业管理
olive branch 橄榄枝
grey income 灰色收入
chain reaction 连锁反应
be armed to teeth 武装到牙齿
domino theory 多米诺骨牌理论
Engel Coefficient 恩格尔系数
black market 黑市
dollar diplomacy 金元外交
pillar industry 支柱产业
an ivory tower 象牙塔
Pandora's box 潘多拉的盒子
a gentleman's agreement 君子协定
human oriented 以人为本

对上述英语短语的汉译采用了直译法，既保留了原文的意思，也保留了原文生动形象的比喻等。虽然原文和译文来自两个不同的语言文化环境，但是汉语读者对译文所蕴含的文化已经非常熟悉。直译时，也需要注意以下问题。

1）直译不是生搬硬套的死译、硬译

直译并非字对字或词对词式的翻译（word for word translation），要根据原文内容和表达形式，将原文译成符合汉语表达习惯和行文规范的译文。

（1）Theory is something, but practice is everying.

【译文】 理论固然重要，但实践更为重要。

【评析】 原文中的"something"和"everything"不可机械地译为"某种东西"或"任何东西"，应以准确表意为前提，进行相应调整。

（2）John has about as much chance of getting a job as of being chosen manager of the company.

【译文】 约翰找到工作的机会和当这个公司经理的机会几乎差不多。

【评析】 原文中的"about as much"不可直译为"几乎许多"。根据原文内容,应译为"几乎并不多"。

2)直译切忌望文生义,警惕"假朋友(false friend)"

英汉两种语言在俗语和谚语的字面意义和指称意义上并不相同,甚至相差甚远。

"He works like a dog.",有人把它译成"他像狗一样干活",这使人联想到狗的顺从、忠诚。其实这仅是对字面含义的理解,它真正的喻义是"He works diligently."(他勤奋地工作。)。看下列短语翻译。

nations in bloom 国际花园城市 (误:花园之国)

United Express 联合航空 (误:联合快递)

bridge the digital 缩小数字鸿沟 (误:过数字鸿沟)

shed labor 裁员/解雇劳动力 (误:流动劳动力)

cellular phone 移动电话 (误:细胞式的电话)

share holding 控股 (误:股票控制)

thorny issue 棘手的问题 (误:艰难的发布)

an old and ragged moon 一弯下弦残月 (误:一轮又老又破的月亮)

white day 吉日 (误:白色的天)

box one's ear 打某人耳光 (误:打某人的耳朵)

fat farm 减肥中心 (误:脂肪农场)

red meat 牛、羊、猪肉 (误:红色的肉)

blue coat 警察 (误:蓝色上衣)

red cap 火车站搬运工 (误:红帽子)

busybody 爱管闲事的人 (误:大忙人)

cock and bull story 无稽之谈/荒诞的故事(误:鸡和牛的故事)

twice told tale 老掉牙的故事 (误:讲过两次的故事)

Indian summer 小阳春(深秋或初冬季节风和日丽的宜人气候;天气回暖)(误:印第安夏天)

babysitter 替人照看孩子的人(误:婴儿座椅)

上面短语的字面意义和指称意义并不完全相同。翻译时，不能望文生义，想当然地翻译，而要去揣摩词义，也要日常积累，养成勤查字典的习惯。

3）利用汉语语言优势

翻译时，常见的两类问题是：①译文语义基本符合原文，但汉语表达欠可读性，或是汉语表达尚有可读性，但译文语义不符合原文；②直译易"信"而不易"顺"，"信"与"顺"并非是对立的，在正确理解原文并充分发挥译入语优势的情况下，两者是可以统一的。例如：

（1）Pressing down the button of the alarm clock, he curled up for a last warm moment under the bedclothes.

【译文 1】 他把闹钟的按钮按下，蜷缩在被子下面，享受最后一刻的温暖。

【译文 2】 他把闹钟的按钮按下，蜷缩在被子下面，享受最后温暖的一刻。

【评析】 译文 1 和译文 2 都是忠实流畅的译文，但是比较"最后一刻的温暖"和"最后温暖的一刻"，显然前者更胜一筹。

（2）It is easy to compress a gas. It is just a matter of reducing the space between the molecules. Like a liquid a gas has no shape，but unlike a liquid it will expand and fill any container it is put in.

【译文 1】 气体是很容易压缩的，这正是压缩分子之间距离的根据。气体和液体一样没有形状，但又不同于液体，气体膨胀时会充满任何盛放它的容器。

【译文 2】 气体很容易压缩，那只不过是缩小分子之间的距离而已。气体和液体一样没有形状，但又不同于液体，因为气体会扩张并充满任何盛放它的容器。

【评析】 译文 1 虽然句子顺畅，但却扭曲了原文的意义，在这里，将"matter"译成"根据"在物理学上是讲不通的，因为"压缩气体也就是减少分子之间的距离"，两者是一回事。"matter"应作"事情、问题"解。译文 2 采用了直译，按照原文的顺序顺译，基本上能表达原文的意义。

鲁迅曾经说："凡是翻译，必须兼顾两面，一则力求其易解，一则保存原作的风姿。"另外，要真正达到钱钟书先生所称道的"化境"——"既能不因语言习惯的差异而露出生硬牵强的痕迹，又能完全保存原有的风味"，译者需要不断锤炼自己的语言，在翻译实践中尽量发挥汉语言的优势。反之也要看到，对于原文中有生命力的表达方式，如有需要和可能，应尽量移植过来，以丰富汉语的词汇和表达。但是，在不可能的情况下，也不要勉为其难，以免弄巧成拙。

4）在翻译中，警惕"翻译腔"

译文表达通顺、忠实是最基本的要求。忠实包括忠实于信息、语气、文体风格。通顺包括造词、句式、呼应、文采，文从句顺，流畅易懂。尤金·奈达在《翻译理论与实践》一书中，专门造了一个词"translationese"（翻译腔）形容翻译的常见病。陆谷孙主编的《英汉大字典》收入了这个词条，将其解释为"表达不流畅、不地道的翻译文体；翻译腔；佶屈聱牙的翻译语言。"

翻译腔是翻译初学者在汉语译文中不知不觉表现出来的一种倾向。由于翻译时所要表达的内容来自外语原文，原文的词语和结构形式先进入大脑，随后被带入译文，造成了译文的翻译腔。例如：

（1）As a husband, he is affectionate.

【译文 1】 作为一个丈夫，他十分深情。

【译文 2】 他是个深情的丈夫。

【评析】 译文1将英语的介词"as"生硬地译为"作为"，保留了英语的句法形式，但这种句法形式在现代汉语中并不常见，明显带有翻译腔。译文2是地道的汉语句子，是对原句更确切的汉译。

（2）We have talked about this issue today.

【译文 1】 我们今天已经讨论过关于这个议题的事了。

【译文 2】 我们今天讨论过这个议题了。

【评析】 译文1生硬地将介词"about"翻译为"关于"，忽略了汉语中"讨论"是及物动词的事实，造成翻译腔。译文2是地道的汉语句子，是对原句更确切的汉译。

（3）When you finish the draft, send it to me.

【译文 1】 当你写完稿子的时候，把它寄给我吧。

【译文 2】 稿子写完了，就寄给我吧。

【评析】 英语小句间的连接必须有连词，但汉语是意合语言，多余的连词往往造成文句不通的现象。因此译文 2 明显比译文 1 更符合汉语的表达习惯。

Versions for Appreciation（译文赏析）

（1）One stone kills two birds.

【译文】 一石击二鸟。

【评析】 仔细研究译文，会发现译文近乎完美的同时，保留了原文的内容和外在形式。译文五个汉字，原文五个单词，意义、词性等方面可谓字字对应。唯一的差异体现在英语有数（number）、格（case）、时（tense）等屈折变化，而汉语译文没有这种表达手段。"To kill two birds with one stone"现在一般译作"一石二鸟"，是由汉语的成语"一箭双雕"仿造而成。

（2）For my parents and I know that if I work hard at my cause, the achievements can be surely made.

【译文】 父母和我知道只要在事业上肯努力，一定会取得成就的。

【评析】 此句译文是按照原文的表达顺序翻译的，译者采取直译的方法使译文符合汉语表意。

（3）Corrupt officials are corrupt officials.

【译文】 贪官就是贪官。

【评析】 试比较"贪官就是贪官"和"贪性难改"。两个译文一个直译，一个意译。直译的译文保留了原文重复的形式和含蓄的语气，而意译的译文则译出了言下之意。相比较，直译的译文无论在形式还是内容上都更加贴近原文。

（4）The sun was coming over the hills. A bass jumped, making a circle in the water. Nick trailed his hand in the water. It felt warm in the sharp chill of the morning.

【译文】 太阳露出山头。一条鲈鱼跳起来,使水面泛起一圈涟漪。尼克把手伸到水里,在清晨凛冽的寒气里,水摸上去很暖和。

【评析】 译文采用了直译法。原文出自海明威的小说《印第安人的营房》。海明威的语言简洁凝练,这段文字中句子简短,省略了所有连词。译文也同样采用了短句,文字简洁,使用朴素而贴切的动词和形容词,很好地传达出了原文的内容和艺术风格。

(5) She was forced to face up to a few unwelcome truths about her family.

【译文】 她不得不正视有关她家的几桩尴尬事。

【评析】 译文基本采用直译,但是译文中舍弃了原文被动语态的形式。这是因为汉语和英语在被动语态的使用上有较大不同,英语中的被动句可译成汉语中的主动语态。

(6) As John loved me, I weep for him; as he was fortunate, I rejoice at it; as he was valiant, I honor him; but as he was ambitious, I slew him. There is tear for his love; joy for his fortune; honor for his valor; and death for his ambition.

【译文】 因为约翰爱我,我为他哭泣;因为他幸运,我为他高兴;因为他英勇,我对他尊崇;但因为他有野心,我就刺杀了他。用眼泪回报他的爱;用欢乐庆祝他的幸运;用尊崇纪念他的英勇;而用刺杀制止他的野心。

【评析】 译文采用了直译法,保留了原文的重复以及排比结构,但同时也充分运用了汉语独特的表达优势。英语句子倾向于多用名词和介词,而现代汉语则是动词占优势,这是现代汉语句法的显著特征之一。原文中第二句使用介词 for 四次,而译文中充分利用汉语语言,将这些介词分别转换成四个动词"回报""庆祝""纪念""制止",短句之间不用任何连接词,纯靠语义上的关联,读来顺畅、自然。

(7) The audiences gave good reactions to the speaker last night.

【译文】 昨晚听众对演讲者反应十分热烈。

【评析】 该句英语是动宾结构的句子,翻译成汉语的时候基本按直译翻译,只是调整了句型,使用了汉语的话题结构,更符合汉语的表达习惯。

第 6 章　Literal and Free Translation in English（直译法与意译法）

Questions for Teacher's Lecture（讲解题）

Translate the following sentences into Chinese.

（1）China-EU economies are strongly complimentary to each other and hence enjoy huge potential for cooperation in trade, investment, science and technology areas.

（2）I saw a girl who talks and looks like your elder sister.

（3）His opinion isn't accepted.

（4）There are plenty of restaurants for those who tire of shopping.

（5）Dawn breaks over the islands, very beautiful in a soft grey light with many clouds. There is a transparency about the light here which cannot be described or painted.

（6）In the late summer of that year we lived in a house in a village that looked across the river and the plain to the mountains.

（7）Rich women for the most part keep themselves busy with innumerable trifles of whose earth shaking importance they are firmly persuaded.

Exercises for Students（练习题）

Translate the following sentences into Chinese.

（1）As a company president, he is competent.

（2）Against this backdrop of knowledge—both the known and the unknown—it is clear that some foreign companies are itching to get across to Asian markets.

（3）In some automated plants the entire production line is controlled by computers.

（4）Most people, when they are left free to fill their own time according to their own choice, are at a loss to think of anything sufficiently pleasant to be worth doing.

（5）China-EU trade and economic cooperation has yielded heartening fruits. The EU is now an important economic and trade partner of China.

（6）As the largest developing country in the world, China is proved to have stable political and social environment, constant economic growth and ever-opening market as well as ever-better market atmosphere.

6.2　Free Translation（意译）

与直译不同，意译不能逐字逐句翻译。通常在翻译句子、词组或更大的意群时使用意译的情况较多，主要原因是意译能更好地处理英语与汉语之间存在的巨大文化差异。从跨文化语言交际和文化交流的角度来看，意译强调的是译入语（即汉语文化体系）和源语（即英语文化体系）的相对独立性。也就是说，意译从意义出发，不拘泥于细节，译文自然流畅即可。

何种情况需要意译呢？看下面两个译文。

He gave his youth to the frontier cause and he came home and gave his wife his old age.

【译文1】　他把青春献给了边疆事业，他回来的时候便把老年给了他的妻子。

【译文2】　他把青春献给了边疆事业，等到回到家里见到妻子的时候，已经是白发苍苍了。

【评析】　译文1的后面部分让人觉得别扭，是在死译。译文2将"...and he came home and gave his wife his old age"改为"等到回到家里见到妻子的时候，已经是白发苍苍了"。译文自然流畅。对比译文1，译文2准确、精妙地传达了原文的含义。

受民族风俗、历史文化等因素的影响，各民族的语言都有其独特的词汇、句法结构和表达方式，译文若直译，有时佶屈聱牙，晦涩难懂，引起歧义，这时就需要采取意译，使译文符合汉语的规范。翻译

第 6 章　Literal and Free Translation in English（直译法与意译法）

时，直译和意译是不可分割的。根据原文的思想内容，能直译就直译，不宜直译时，应采用意译。

英语中有大量具有鲜明文化色彩的词语，如俚语、俗语、习语、典故等，其字面意义并不同于真正所指的意义，它与语言背后的文化背景紧密相关。例如："He is a blue-eyed boy."（他是一个宠儿。），并不能译为"蓝眼睛的男孩"。又如："as rich as Croesus"意译为"十分富有"。Croesus 是公元 6 世纪小亚细亚吕底亚国王，他的国家有一种特别的矿——"银金矿"，一种金和银混合的矿物，当地人用这种"白色的金子"制成了世界上最早的钱币。货币的发明促进贸易的繁荣，吕底亚王国强盛一时，十分富有。如直译为"像科里瑟斯一样富有"，就不如"十分富有"简单明了。

所以说，语用意义与文化因素有着相当密切的关系，不同的文化会赋予相同的对象以不同的联想意义。以动物为例，不同联想意义的产生有时与动物的本性有关，例如：鸡、绵羊、山羊、奶牛等这几种动物，在汉语中，绵羊会让人联想到"懦弱温顺"，其他几种动物并没有特别的联想意义。而在英语中它们分别有以下联想意义："胆怯，懦弱"（chicken hearted）；"驯服，腼腆，羞怯"（sheepish）；"好色，淫荡"（goatish）和"粗壮邋遢，不清洁"（You smell cow!）等。例如：

（1）He was a rat in the revolutionary ranks.

【译文】　他是革命队伍中的变节者。

【评析】　此句里的"rat"有特别的寓意，不是字面意思"鼠"。

（2）He was outlived by his wife.

【译文】　他不如他妻子活得长。

【评析】　这句若直译为"他被他妻子活过了。"显然不符合汉语的表达习惯，这时要摆脱原文结构的束缚，采用地道的汉语表达。

（3）These foreign tourists saw the lions in Beijing yesterday.

【译文】　这些外国游客昨天游览了北京的名胜。

【评析】　句子中的"lions"已成为北京名胜的象征。

意译时需要防止以下几点。

1）避免胡乱翻译

意译并非胡译、乱译，不可以辞害意。例如：

（1）Theory is something, but practice is everything.

【译文 1】 实践之重，重于泰山／实践之高，高于一切。

【译文 2】 理论固然重要，但实践更为重要。

【评析】 两个译文中，译文 1 貌似意译，实为乱译，以辞害意。译文 2 才是忠实于原文的译法。

（2）Times are changed with him who marries: there are no more by path meadows, where you may innocently linger, but the road lies long and straight and dusty to the grave.

【译文 1】 人一旦结婚，情况就会发生变化，路边不再有如茵的草地任你天真地徜徉，取而代之的是长路漫漫，尘埃茫茫，一直通向坟墓。

【译文 2】 结婚的人就不同了，再也不能流连芳草三心二意，只能从一而终始终不渝。

【评析】 译文 2 中"流连芳草""从一而终"等词显然是译者引申过度。意译并不等同于信口开河，不着边际的翻译。胡译、乱译同死译、硬译一样都是不科学的翻译态度。翻译实践证明，大量英语句子的汉译都要采取意译法。如果把意译理解为凭主观臆想来理解原文，可能会不分析原文结构，只看词面意义，自己编造句子，造成乱译。

2）习语和俗语的翻译

平时应注意积累英语中的习语和俗语。我们在上文中讲到，英语中有许多与文化相关的习语和俗语，初学者如果掉以轻心，往往会犯一些低级错误。例如：

（1）They had been enemies for ages, but after a fight they buried the hatchet.

【译文】 他们敌对了很长时间，但打了一仗以后就休战和好了。

【评析】 这句中的"bury the hatchet"，如果直译成"把斧子埋了"，势必令读者感到莫名其妙。这里将"bury the hatchet"译作"休战和好"恰到好处。

（2）He met the congressmen in secret to exert backstairs influence.

【译文】 他暗中与议员会面施加幕后影响。

【评析】 这个句子中"exert backstairs influence"表示"施加幕后影响"。此处，如果按照字面译为"施加后楼梯的影响"，会让读者感到不知所云。

3）灵活运用直译和意译

译者应根据作品的语境、场景、情调、表达习惯等准确理解原文，灵活地选用直译和意译，用恰当的语言传达出原文的内容。例如：

（1）Better is as stubborn as a donkey.

【译文】 比特非常固执。

【评析】 这里的"donkey"（驴子）在英语中暗含愚蠢之人的意思，一提到"donkey"就会使人联想到愚蠢的人。由于不同文化赋予同一对象以不同的联想意义，该句应选择意译。

（2）Now, it is very convenient that shoppers would never be more than a mouse click from the best deals.

【译文】 现在很方便，购物者只需点击一下鼠标即可做成一笔最好的交易。

【评析】 如果直译为"购物者离最好的交易再也不会超过点击一下鼠标的距离。"看似保留了原文形式，但却不能忠实于原文的内容，相比之下，此句的译文显然更加忠实、流畅。

（3）The man is very lazed, so he is as poor as a church mouse.

【译文】 这个男人很懒，因此他现在是一贫如洗。

【评析】 原句采用了simile（明喻），如果保留这个形式译成"他像教堂里的老鼠一样穷"就显得粗俗、滑稽、不知所云，而且不能传达出原句的本意。这时采用意译为佳。

（4）Great birth is a very poor dish at table.

【译文】 出身高贵不当饭吃。

【评析】 如果直译，读者会很费解，所以意译为"出身高贵不当饭吃"。原文说"dish"，译文说"当饭吃"，虽不是形似，却是神似，原文与译文可谓有异曲同工之处。

（5）My father was a loyal member of his party and always voted the straight ticket.

【译文】 我爸爸忠于他的党派，而且总是把票投给他那个党派的候选人。

【评析】 如果直译成"我爸爸忠于他的党派，而且总是直接投票。"不符合汉语的逻辑，需要补出投票的对象才能使汉语使用者一目了然。所以译文采取了意译法。

（6）Mary wanted to hit the sack and get some Z's.

【译文】 玛丽想要睡会儿觉。

【评析】 原文"hit the sack"是指"去睡觉"，"get some Z's"是指"睡会儿觉"。所以此句只能采用意译法。

（7）Inexperienced people get stars in their eyes when they think of changing the world.

【译文】 没有经验的人一想到改变世界就迫不及待。

【评析】 这句话如果直译成"没有经验的人一想到改变世界就会眼睛里面冒星星"，中国人很难读懂其隐含的意义，前半部分直译后半部分意译就很好地解决了这个问题。

（8）He wanted to run, but that would be the worst thing he could do.

【译文】 他真想跑，但那是他能做的最糟糕的事。

【评析】 从原文的内容和语言结构来看，不需要意译，直译就能把原文的意思清楚地表达出来。

（9）In recent years, the cross-cutting issues of economics and social aspects have beconе more and more important.

【译文】 近年来，经济和社会发展之间的协调问题变得越来越重要。

【评析】 从原文表达的意思和语言结构来看，没有任何难点或问题需要引申和解释，按照字面意思直译就可以清楚地把原文内容表达出来。

第 6 章　Literal and Free Translation in English（直译法与意译法）

Questions for Teacher's Lecture（讲解题）

Translate the following sentences into Chinese.

（1）EU enterprises enjoy advanced equipment, technologies and management expertise in traditional sectors such as machinery, automobiles, chemical industry and electronics and also service sectors such as banking and insurance industries.

（2）Knowledge is a comfortable and necessary retreat and shelter for us in an advanced age, and if we do not plant it while young, it will give us no shade when we grow old.

（3）I'm delighted to see that EU enterprises are giving more confidence to the Chinese market under the background of global economic recession.

（4）Shakespeare put his hometown on the map.

（5）John would not come out of his shell and talk to others at the party.

（6）He has a rough-and-ready character.

（7）After the failure of his last novel, his reputation stands on slippery ground.

（8）I am afraid she is too far from the cradle for you.

Exercises for Students（练习题）

Translate the following sentences into Chinese.

（1）I would like to note that there are a large number of small and medium-sized enterprises in the EU which all have their unique technological features.

（2）He got into trouble when he paid his bills with rubber checks.

（3）On a rainy day the children sometimes ran their mother ragged.

（4）He really has the heart in the right place to serve the people.

（5）The naughty boy was making a mouth in the classroom.

6.3　Literal and Free Translation of Practical Writings
　　　（几种实用文体的直译和意译）

1. 商标翻译

　　在世界经济加速一体化的商品经济时代，外国的商品要进入中国市场，中国的商品也要打入国际市场。这就涉及商标翻译的问题。商标命名往往源于特定的文化，反映不同的文化习俗与文化特征。商标是产品的"黄金名片"，它有宣传、促销的作用。因此做好商标翻译十分重要。

　　从语言形式看，商标的语言简洁易懂，但要让受众知之、好之、乐之，达到音、形、意的完美统一，也并非易事。

　　商标翻译的方法有音译法、意译法、谐音取意法、改译法、转译法、借用法等。

　1）音译法

　　音译即把源语商标中的音用发音相似或相同的词语表现出来。若源语商标无具体含义，多采用音译法。采用音译法的最大优点是可以保留原商标名的音韵之美，体现商品的异国情调或正宗特色，给消费者留下深刻的印象。尤其在国际市场有许多商品的商标是以企业或商品的创办人、发明人或商品产地命名，译名一般采用约定俗成的音译，以免引起混乱和消费者误解，影响产品销售。常见的音译商标有：

　　HUAWEI　华为

　　VOLVO　沃尔沃

　　Huang Shan　黄山牌香烟

　　Rolls-Royce　劳斯莱斯

　　Midea　美的（电器）

　　CHUNGHWA　中华牌香烟

　　MOUTAI　茅台酒

　　YOUNGER　雅戈尔

　　NOKIA　诺基亚

　　Fenbid　芬必得

2）意译法

在商标翻译中，意译法是最常见的翻译方法，翻译时直接考虑商标词汇的含义，转化为相应的英语或汉语词汇，这种翻译方法立足于本国文化，侧重文化内涵。常见的用意译法翻译的商标有：

Volkswagen 大众

Microsoft 微软

3）谐音取义法

谐音取义法又称谐音双关法。汉语里有很多同音异义的字，翻译时，经过精心琢磨和推敲后，应选择发音响亮，有意境的字。产于美国的饮料 Coca-Cola 进入中国市场的时候，曾有人将它翻译成"口渴口辣"。这个品牌名会让消费者联想到干涩无味，难以下咽的感觉，让消费者产生反感。后来采用谐音取义法，将它译成"可口可乐"，既保留了音节，又能让消费者产生好感。

Versions for Appreciation（译文赏析）

（1）Honeyplanting

【译文】 植蜜雅

【评析】 这是一个化妆品的商标。植物配方，与你"蜜"不可分，体现了产品清幽淡雅的特点。此商标采用了意译法。

（2）Tide

【译文】 汰渍

【评析】 "汰"在古文中是洗的意思，在吴语区，"汰"字如今在口语中仍然使用，"渍"即污迹。译名在发音上与原品名谐音，同时意义又紧扣产品性质（洗衣粉），可谓佳译。

（3）Mimore

【译文】 米蔓

【评析】 这是一个糯米商标。其实，它的英文名字是"mirth"与"more"的组合，含有欢笑、欢乐的意思。此商标采用了音译法。

（4）Safeguard

【译文】 舒肤佳

【评析】 中文与原文发音相似，同时中文字面意思就是"使皮肤舒适，保持最佳状态"，突出了这种香皂的功能。

（5）BENZ

【译文】 奔驰

【评析】 奔驰1号是世界上第一辆以内燃机为动力的汽车，在中国奔驰已经成为高档轿车的代名词。中文译名体现了该车的优越性能，使人联想到乘坐该车奔腾驰骋的感觉。

4）改译法

改译实际上是重新命名，换一个联想意义好且能突出产品特点的名称。改译既不是音译，也不是意译，而是完全突破原来的英文商标，从市场的传播需要出发，确定一个品牌名称。

（1）Head & Shoulders

【译文】 海飞丝

【评析】 原译为"海德仙度斯"，后来改译为"海飞丝"，既优美，又体现了产品的特色。

（2）Citibank

【译文】 花旗银行

【评析】 原译为"零售银行"，后来改译为"花旗银行"，表意更清楚，也有一种鲜明的特色。

（3）Sprite

【译文】 雪碧

【评析】 原译为"斯普赖特""斯比来特"，以及"小妖精""调皮鬼"，该商品广告初次出现在中国香港，产品销售不佳。后来改译为"雪碧"，给人以冰凉解渴的感觉，体现了饮料产品的特性，消费者乐意接受。

5）转译法和借用法

转译法主要应用于来自日本的产品商标，如同翻译日语中的地名一样。日语商标译为英语时，采用音译的方法，而再从英语译为汉语时，则须使用日语中的汉字。借用法是直接采用照搬原名的办法，方便、简单。

第 6 章　Literal and Free Translation in English（直译法与意译法）

　　随着我国加大对外开放力度，外国品牌纷纷涌入中国，有些商标来不及译，有些商标难译，而更多的商家认为原名不必译，追求"洋味"的人士以及一些新闻媒体偏爱使用外文名称，于是出现许多直接借用源语公司名称或品牌名称的现象。

　　商标翻译与树立产品品牌、赢得市场竞争有着很大的关系。商标翻译是一种跨文化的交际形式。所以，汉译商标首先要尊重和把握源语国家的民族文化、风俗习惯，同时结合商品特征，反映商品信息，使译名优美，增强消费者的购买欲。

Questions for Teacher's Lecture（讲解题）

Translate the following brand names into Chinese.

（1）Transcend

（2）Micron

（3）Yamaha

（4）Rebec

（5）Kingston

（6）Lux

（7）Goldlion

（8）Starbucks

（9）Warrior

（10）Moon Rabbit

Exercises for Students（练习题）

Translate the following baand names into Chinese.

（1）Intel

（2）Tesla

（3）Neon

（4）SanDisk

（5）Clean & Clear

（6）Mickey Mouse

（7）Nippon Paint

（8）Cloud and Mountain

（9）Calling Spring Flower/Primrose

（10）Golden Cock

2. 广告语翻译

英语中的"广告"（advertising）一词源于拉丁语"advertere"，意为"唤起大众对某事物的注意；向公众介绍商品、服务内容等的一种宣传方式"。

在经济全球化的今天，各国之间的交流日益密切，商品广告是连接商品和消费者之间的一座桥梁。

从文体上看，英文广告多为口语体，少见书面体。具体有以下特点。

1）词汇简单化和创新化

英语广告经常选用单音节或者字母数较少的简短动词。例如，用 ease 代替 relieve，用 show 代替 display 或 reveal 等，英语广告中多用缩略词，所有格's 的出现频率比 of 结构要高。同时，由于复合词和前后缀构词方法灵活简便，这种形式在英语广告中也大量出现。在词汇方面，广告中还大量使用褒义词，让商品在消费者的心目中留下正面、美好的形象。

2）翻译句型简单化、口语化

广告需要有极强的可读性，让消费者很快产生深刻的印象。广告语句简短，大量使用省略句，便于唤起消费者的注意力。并列句、疑问句和祈使句在英语广告中也备受青睐。例如：A great way to fly !（飞跃万里，超越一切！）；Luggage that cooperates.（行李有我）。

3）用修辞格翻译

修辞格的使用可增强广告语言的生动性、可读性和吸引力，是广告最为显著的特点之一。广告中的修辞格常用双关、比喻、拟人、夸张、对比、重复、押韵、头韵等。例如：A diamond lasts forever.（钻石恒久远，一颗永流传。），这个广告用了夸张的手法，引起消费者的好奇和兴趣。

广告语就是品牌的眼睛，助人理解品牌内涵。广告语言要准确自然，传达广告真实信息，反对虚假宣传。其次，广告语言要利用各种修辞手段和句式变化使译文简洁、生动，让消费者印象深刻、过目不忘。

广告翻译常用直译法、意译法。

直译法

广告语常见的翻译方法是直译法，译文尽量保留原句的句法和修辞特点，努力再现原文的形式、内容和风格。例如：

（1）Quality never goes out of style.（李维斯服装）

【译文】 质量与风格共存。

（2）Wining the hearts of the world.（法国航空）

【译文】 赢取天下心。

（3）Where there is road, there is Redflag.（红旗牌轿车）

【译文】 车到山前必有路，有路必有红旗车。

（4）Let's make things better.（飞利浦电器）

【译文】 让我们做得更好。

（5）Poetry in motion, dancing closing to me.（丰田汽车）

【译文】 动态的诗，向我舞近。

（6）Advancement through technology.（奥迪汽车）

【译文】 突破科技，启迪未来。

（7）You press the button, we do the rest.（柯达相机）

【译文】 你只需按快门，其余的我们来做。

（8）Tide's in, dirt's out.（汰渍洗衣粉）

【译文】 汰渍到，污垢逃。

（9）Be good to yourself. Fly Emirates.（阿联酋航空）

【译文】 纵爱自己，纵横万里。

意译法

英汉两种语言在词义、结构、文化等各个方面的差异，导致有些情况根本无法直译，尤其是在修辞格方面，直译会让人费解。在这种情况下需采用意译，例如：

（1）Trust us for life.（友邦保险）

【译文】 财政稳健，信守一生。

（2）Good to the last drop.（麦斯威尔咖啡）

【译文】 滴滴香浓，意犹未尽。

Versions for Appreciation（译文赏析）

（1）Wear our jeans, present your cool.（李维斯牛仔裤）

【译文】 不同的裤，相同的酷。

【评析】 这则广告语在结构方面保留了原文的对偶，但在意思方面采用意译法，似乎比原广告词更胜一筹，不仅译出了题眼"cool"，同时采用谐音（裤－酷）、对比（不同－相同）的修辞手法。

（2）Connecting People.（诺基亚）

【译文】 科技以人为本。

【评析】 这是一个典型的意译广告语，如果直译为"连接人们"就有点不知所云了。译文很好地体现了诺基亚的科技属性。

（3）To me, the past is black and white, but the future is always color.（轩尼诗酒）

【译文】 对我而言，过去平淡无奇；而未来，却是绚烂缤纷。

【评析】 原文使用了借代的修辞手法，用颜色来指代过去和未来的生活，很自然地形成了一个鲜明的对比。倘若将"black and white"和"color"直译成"黑色和白色"和"彩色"，会令人费解，相反译者使用意译法，用了汉语的两个成语"平淡无奇"和"绚烂缤纷"。

（4）Mosquito Bye Bye Bye.（雷达牌驱虫剂）

【译文】 蚊子杀杀杀。

【评析】 这则广告可谓已经深入人心。译文一方面采用意译，使用译入语的习惯表达，用三个"杀"来代替三个"bye"，另一方面，译文完美移植了原文的外在形式，虽为意译，但是广告效果却是相同的。

（5）Time is what you make of it.（斯沃奇手表）

【译文】 天长地久。

【评析】 斯沃奇手表的特点是经久耐用，意译的译文版本更适合中国文化对好手表的理解。

Questions for Teacher's Lecture（讲解题）

Translate the following slogans into Chinese.

（1）Focus on life.

（2）Talk global, pay local.

（3）Ugly is only skin deep.

（4）A Mars a day keeps you work, rest and play.

（5）Impossible made possible.

（6）The globe brings you the world in a single copy.

Exercises for Students（练习题）

Translate the following slogans into Chinese.

（1）The art of writing.

（2）Take Toshiba, take the world.

（3）One warrior in the pass and ten thousand lose heart.

（4）My Paris in a perfume.

3. 影视剧名称翻译

影视作品名称的翻译要尽量考虑到它的艺术和商业效果。片名翻译要做到简单易记，雅俗共赏，传情达意，并应与其内容吻合，传达主题信息，吸引观众，增加票房。

在翻译过程中，要考虑到影视节目是一种文化性与商业性兼具的艺术形式。片名是影视作品的商标和广告，要引起观众的心理认同，使其产生观看欲望。影视片名翻译有音译法、直译法、意译法等。

1)音译法

影视作品片名大多以主人公、背景、主题、线索剧情为来源,很多片名本身为人名、地名这样的专有名词。在不致引起译入语文化曲解的前提下,可直接将其音译,例如:

Shining	《闪灵》
Hannibal	《汉尼拔》
Harry Potter and the Sorcerer's Stone	《哈利·波特与魔法石》
Simone	《西蒙尼》
Troy	《特洛伊》
Tarzan	《泰山》
Notting Hill	《诺丁山》
Rocky	《洛基》
Hamlet	《哈姆雷特》/《王子复仇记》

2)直译法

直译法是最常见的译法。在不违背影视作品的情节、内容且不引起错误联想的前提下,直译法可以原汁原味地再现原作风貌。例如:

Sound of Music	《音乐之声》
The Silence of the Lambs	《沉默的羔羊》
The Princess Diaries	《公主日记》
The Godfather	《教父》
Windtalkers	《风语者》
Four Weddings and a Funeral	《四个婚礼和一个葬礼》
Message in a Bottle	《瓶中信》
The Weather Man	《气象先生》
Growing Pains	《成长的烦恼》
Prison Break	《越狱》
Pulp Fiction	《低俗小说》
Babel	《通天塔》
A Farewell to Arms	《永别了,武器》
The Old Man and the Sea	《老人与海》

第 6 章 Literal and Free Translation in English（直译法与意译法）

Dances with Wolves　　　　　　　《与狼共舞》

3）意译法

在片名的翻译过程中，为了让电影更好地适应本土市场，必要时可以将影片名根据电影内容做些改动。意译法以原片名为基础，结合影片内容做适当的润饰。译者在综合、分析、理解原片片名、内容、风格、情节的基础上，对片名进行加工，将它译成能反映原片特点的译名。采用意译法翻译的影视名称，译名会有原名的影子。例如：

Always	《天长地久》
Spiderman	《蜘蛛侠》
Bathing Beauty	《出水芙蓉》
Thelma and Louis	《末路狂花》
Speed	《生死时速》
Amadeus	《上帝的宠儿》
Save the Last Dance	《舞出一片天》
Scent of a Woman	《闻香识女人》
Entrapment	《偷天陷阱》
Green Card	《绿卡情缘》
Love Me Tenderly	《铁汉柔肠》
Hurlyburly	《浮世男女》
Sister Act	《修女也疯狂》
Next	《关键下一秒》
Chicken Little	《四眼天鸡》
Something's Gotta Give	《爱是妥协》
Thirteen	《芳龄十三》

Versions for Appreciation（译文赏析）

（1）Gone with the Wind

【译文】《飘》/《乱世佳人》

【评析】 本作品的作者为美国作家玛格丽特·米切尔,她是美国现代著名的女作家,1937她因长篇小说《飘》获得普利策奖,1949年遇车祸罹难。她短暂的一生并未留下太多的作品,但一部《飘》足以奠定她在世界文学史上不可动摇的地位。根据这部小说改编的电影《乱世佳人》,其译名也是汉英译名中的经典之作,展现了影片中那战乱纷飞、颠覆传统的时代。

(2) Forrest Gump

【译文】《阿甘正传》

【评析】 这部影片的译名借用鲁迅先生的《阿Q正传》,点出了这部电影是人物传记题材,译成"甘"又考虑到原片名,点出主人公的姓氏。"阿甘"这种带有中国式特色的名字深入人心。

Questions for Teacher's Lecture(讲解题)

Translate the following movie names into Chinese.

(1) The Da Vinci Code

(2) Saving Private Ryan

(3) City of Angels

(4) Great Expectations

(5) Meet Joe Black

(6) Bridges of Madison County

(7) How Green Was My Valley

(8) Head Over Heels

Exercises for Students(练习题)

Translate the following movie names into Chinese.

(1) Casablanca

(2) Legally Blonde

(3) Addicted to Love

(4) *Rain Man*
(5) *Stuart Little*
(6) *Happened One Night*
(7) *Star Wars*
(8) *Walk in the Clouds*

第7章

Cultural Consciousness in English-Chinese Translation
（英译汉中的文化意识）

英语中的"文化（culture）"一词源于拉丁语 *cultura*，其本意是耕耘、耕作土地，种植、栽培庄稼，培育、饲养家畜等。这种含义今天在"农业"（agriculture）和"园艺"（horticulture）两词中仍然保留了下来。

社会学家们普遍认为，文化是人和自然、人与世界全部复杂关系种种表现形式的总和。英国人类学家泰勒（Edward Burnett Tylor）认为广义的文化包括知识、信仰、艺术、伦理道德、法律、风俗等。由此可见，文化是一个有机整体，包括工具和消费品、各种社会群体的制度宪纲、人们的观念和记忆、信仰和习俗。

语言和文化具有相互依存的密切关系，不同民族有着不同文化。翻译不仅要着眼于语言转换，还要透过语言表层，了解其深层内涵和文化含义。著名的美国翻译理论家尤金·奈达在《语言、文化与翻译》一书中指出："语言在文化中的作用以及文化对词义、习语含义的影响如此带有普遍性，以至于在不仔细考虑语言文化背景的情况下，任何文本都无法恰当地加以理解。"

7.1 Differences in Cultural Consciousness（文化意识的差异）

1. 历史文化和典故造成的文化差异与翻译

历史文化就是特定的历史发展进程和社会遗产的沉淀所形成的文化。不同的民族拥有不同的历史和社会遗产。英语中有一词 bridal shower，按照英美国家的传统习俗，bridal shower 是指新娘出嫁前家人为她举行的茶话会（high tea party），因此译为"待嫁酒会"更恰当。英国人说 between the devil and the sea 是表达进退维谷的意思。各国的习语典故所表达的意义并不相同。

英语习语和典故大多源于古希腊、罗马神话或一些经典文学作品，也包括《圣经》。历史典故和一个民族的历史背景、经济、生活环境、心理状态等是密切相关的。因此，通过典故可以了解一个民族的历史文化和风俗民情。

第 7 章　Cultural Consciousness in English-Chinese Translation（英译汉中的文化意识）

英语中的习语和典故

Experience does it（经验使人聪明）；Extremes meet（物极必反）；Fight fire with fire（以毒攻毒），Fire proves gold，adversity proves man（逆境识英雄）；Achille's heel（致命弱点）；like a Trojan（英勇顽强）；King Stork（专制君主）；a dog in the manger（占着茅坑不拉屎）；be not Hamlet（绝不犹豫）；extremes of fortune（盛衰荣枯）等。

汉语中的习语和典故

对牛弹琴（play the lute to a cow）；兵贵神速（Speed is precious in war.）；三顾茅庐（make three calls at the thatched cottage）；东施效颦（ugly woman trying to imitate a famous beauty）；负荆请罪（carry a rod on one's back and ask for punishment）；狐假虎威（the fox assuming the majesty of the tiger）；金戈铁马（golden dagger-axe and armoured horses）；同舟共济（The people in the same boat should help each other.）；锲而不舍（work with perseverance）；十年树木，百年树人（It takes ten years to grow trees but a hundred years to rear people.），运筹帷幄（sit within a command tent and devise strategies）等。

Versions for Appreciation（译文赏析）

（1）He always works his fingers to the bone.

【译文】　他总是竭尽全力去工作。

【评析】　句子中的"to the bone"意为"到极点、极端"。由"bone"构成的习语很多，例如：cut to the bone（削减），feel it in one's bones（预感某事一定会发生），one bone one flesh（夫妻一体）等。

（2）The collective reserve funds will be earmarked for the environmental protection.

【译文】　这笔集体资金是专供保护环境用的。

【评析】　本句"earmark"是用来表示专有权的。在西方历史上，农民习惯在牛、羊耳朵上打烙印，标明主人，以防被盗。现代英语中把这个意思引申一下，意为"指定/供……使用"。

（3）Birds can be caught by a net at the door.

【译文】 门可罗雀。

【评析】 门可罗雀讲的是汉朝翟公当廷尉时,有很多宾客前来拜访,塞满门庭。当他被罢官之后,就没有宾客再来了,门口冷落得都可以张网捕鱼了。当翟公复官之后,由于宾客又来拜访他,他便在门口写了一张纸条,门客便不好意思地走了。

(4) All the tickets have been sold for the singer's performance in London this week, and the public believed that will be her swan song.

【译文】 这个歌手本周在伦敦演出的票都售罄了,因为大家相信这会是她的告别演出。

【评析】 这句中使用了一个典故,即"天鹅在临死时才会唱歌"。而在中文翻译中,"swan song"被翻译为"告别演出"。这一翻译充分体现了文学创作者深邃的文学情感,极具文学气息。

(5) Firing him is like killing the goose that lays the golden egg. He's the best employee in the company.

【译文】 解雇他就是杀鸡取卵。他可是公司里最好的员工。

【评析】 这句话中的"killing the goose that lays the golden egg"涉及一个西方寓言,讲述的是一位农夫的故事。农夫梦想发财,在得到会下金蛋的鹅之后仍然不满足,为了得到更多财富,杀了鹅取金蛋,结果却大失所望。这个寓言故事主要是告诉人们不要过于贪婪。

2. 地域风俗造成的文化差异与翻译

不同地域的民族对某一特定事物的认识也会有所不同。特定的地理环境造就了特定的文化形式,产生特定的表达方式。不同的环境造就了不同的语言、知识、信仰、人生观、价值观、思维方式、道德和风俗。翻译的错误常常出现在词义选择上,因为恰如其分地表达源语词语的意义很难。词义的褒贬、概念的虚实、所指的抽象和具体概念以及修辞、语体和风格等都会被一个民族的生活习惯、思维特征和语言规律所影响。例如:

spend money like water(挥金如土)

go by the board(落空、失败)

burn one's boats(破釜沉舟,自断后路)

第 7 章　Cultural Consciousness in English-Chinese Translation（英译汉中的文化意识）

all at sea（不知所措）

earn one's bread（赚钱糊口）

butter up（讨好，巴结）

big cheese（大人物）

have jam on it（好上加好）

a piece of cake（小菜一碟）

Versions for Appreciation（译文赏析）

（1）There are plenty of more fish in the sea.

【译文】　大海里有的是鱼。

【评析】　有人在恋爱中失意时，中国人可能就用"天涯何处无芳草"来表示安慰，而英国人则用"大海里有的是鱼"来表示安慰。

（2）A good sailor is not known when the sea is calm and water is fair.

【译文】　天气晴朗和大海平静时是看不出一个好水手的。

【评析】　比喻在严峻考验之下，才能显示出谁是强者。英语多用此句表达这个意思，而汉语则说"疾风知劲草，路遥知马力。"这就是两种语言表达方式的不同。

（3）In the evening, after a huge tea, including a big Christmas cake covered with a frosting as sweet as candy and as smooth as pudding, the family will probably sit round the fire eating nuts, sweets and fruit, talking or watching television, or playing party games.

【译文】　晚上吃茶点之后，还有一盒圣诞大蛋糕，蛋糕上的糖霜甜如蜜果，滑如布丁。然后，全家人可坐在壁炉旁，一边吃干果和水果，一边聊天、看电视或做集体游戏。

【评析】　此句翻译要注意两点。第一，"tea"不可译为"茶"，应该译为"茶点"，这就反映了不同的民族风俗文化。"tea"在此处指的是 a small meal of bread and butter and cakes eaten between 4：00 PM. and 5：00 PM（下午吃的点心，尤其在英国文化里是指下午 4 点至 5 点之间吃的小餐，有面包、奶油和蛋糕）。第二，"fire"原意是"火、篝火"，此处译为"壁炉"。外国人喜欢在客厅里设一个壁炉,这是他们的生活习惯。

(4) The CEO really had egg on his face after he went on stage to demonstrate the new product and couldn't get it to work.

【译文】 首席执行官上台演示新产品,但他自己却不会用,真的是出丑了。

【评析】 "have egg on one's face"直译是"脸上有鸡蛋"。西方文化中向某人的脸上扔鸡蛋的意思就是"羞辱某人,令某人丢脸",汉语中没有这种表达,因此译为"出丑"更为合适。

(5) One eye-witness is better than ten hear-says.

【译文】 百闻不如一见。

【评析】 这是一句谚语。 如果词义联想不当,直译为"一次目睹胜过十次耳闻",则没有完全体现原文的含义。在英语中,ten 除了表示具体数字"十"之外,还用以泛指"多",所以,译为"百闻不如一见"更为贴切。

(6) It is impossible to overestimate the value of the invention.

【译文】 这项发明的价值极高,不容低估。

【评析】 这是一个体现英语典型逆向思维的双重否定结构。如果直译为"过高估计这项发明的价值是不可能的",则与原文的意思大相径庭。

(7) If you ever think he is lazy,think again.

【译文】 如果你认为他懒的话,那你就错了。

【评析】 如果直译为:"如果你认为他懒的话,再想一想吧。"从表面上看十分忠实原文,但由于忽略了在特定环境下英语习惯表达的特点,实际上没有将原文的真正意思译出来。

3. 宗教信仰造成的文化差异与翻译

宗教文化不仅影响着社会的经济、政治、科学、哲学、文化艺术,而且潜在、长久地影响着人类的思想与行为。

英语文化是深植于基督教文化之中的,《圣经》在整个西方文明的形成和发展中起了不可估量的作用。在我国影响极为深远的是佛教文化。两种文化在思维习惯上、语言表达形式上、词汇意象和含义上都有着自己的特色。与中国宗教文化相关的词汇、习语有"极""阴阳""听天由命""救人一命胜造七级浮屠""做一天和尚撞一天钟""闲时不烧香,临时抱佛脚"等。而在西方,与宗教相关的习语有 God helps those who help themselves(自助者天助也),not to know a man from Adam(素不相识),separate the sheep from the goats(分清良莠,区别善恶)等。

Versions for Appreciation(译文赏析）

(1) John is just a doubting Thomas. He won't believe what anybody tells him.

【译文】 约翰这个人太多疑了,任何人说什么他都不信。

【评析】 这句话中的 "doubting Thomas" 源于《圣经》。Thomas 是耶稣的十二门徒之一,此人生性多疑。因此英语中使用 "doubting Thomas" 表示多疑之人。

(2) What will it be when the increase of yearly production is brought to a complete stop ? Here is the vulnerable place, the heel of Achilles, for capitalistic.

【译文】 要是每年的生产完全停止,情形又将是怎样呢?这里正是资本主义的阿喀琉斯之踵,它的致命弱点。

【评析】 句中的 "the heel of Achilles" 来自希腊神话。相传阿喀琉斯年幼时,他母亲把他浸在冥河里,使他不为刀剑所伤,但因他的脚后跟是其母手握之处,没有浸到水里,所以他终因此处受到剑伤而死。

(3) There is not an iota of truth in the story.

【译文】 这个故事完全是虚构出来的。

【评析】 句中的 "not an iota of" 出自《新约·马太福音》第 5 章:"律法的一点一画都不能废去,都要成全。""iota"是希腊字母表中第 9 个字母"Ι"的名称,它有时可以写作一短横置于其他字母之上。遗漏这一点点对发音并无什么影响,但按规则不能减少。由此,在英语中遗留下来这个成语,表示 not a bit of, not one jot or little, not at all

等意思。

（4）He was in the seventh heaven last night.

【译文】 他昨天晚上欣喜若狂。

【评析】 许多人望文生义，把"in the seventh heaven"同"升天""死"的概念联系起来。其实这条成语同宗教有关。在基督教中，七重天是指上帝和天使居住的天国最高层。言下之意，人能身居天国最高层，与上帝同住，自然是非常愉快的。这条成语的释义是"in a state of great happiness or contentment"。

（5）Maliya desires to go back home and put on her Sunday best because she is going out with a very good friend to try that new French restaurant which they hear is so good.

【译文】 玛利亚很想回家去换件体面衣服。因为她要跟一个非常好的朋友一起去那个新开张的法国饭馆。听说那是家非常好的饭馆。

【评析】 此处"Sunday best"可能会引起理解困难。这个表达也是源于基督教的风俗。在西方国家，人们星期天去教堂的时候，总是穿得非常正式，非常漂亮。所以，"Sunday best"就是一个人最漂亮的衣服。

（6）In the discontent of his subjects, the ruler saw the handwriting on the wall.

【译文】 统治者从他臣民的不满情绪中看到了不祥之兆。

【评析】 "the handwriting or finger on the wall"的字面意思是"墙上的文字（或手指）"，实际意义是指"不祥之兆，大祸临头"。这个习语出自《圣经·旧约》。有一次古巴比伦（Babylonian）的国王伯沙撒（Belshazzar）正在宫殿里设宴纵饮时，突然，不知从哪里出现了一个神秘的手指，当着国王的面，在王宫与灯台相对的粉墙上写了四个奇怪的单词，后来人们叫来了被掳的犹太预言家但以理，才明白了这几个字的意思就是大难临头。果然，当夜伯沙撒被杀，由62岁的玛代人大利乌取而代之。后来"The handwriting/finger on the wall"就有了以下含义："a sign or warning of impending disaster；a sign that sth. bad will happen；a feeling that one's number is up"。

第 7 章 Cultural Consciousness in English-Chinese Translation（英译汉中的文化意识）

Questions for Teacher's Lecture（讲解题）

Translate the following sentences into Chinese.

（1）I believe it was first gun that had been fired there since the creation of the world.

（2）A large number of American radio stations operate in red.

（3）He always buries his head in the sand.

（4）Mr. Li has his head screwed on the right way in dealing with everything.

（5）Mary has the heart in the right place to help others.

（6）It appeared to be a real bargain, but I smelled something fishy because the man was in such a hurry to sell it. I was right—later on I found out the car was stolen.

（7）The manager always works hard in the company for digging his heels.

（8）When I say Chinese food, I mean Chinese food.

（9）"It is true that the enemy won the battle, but theirs is but a Pyrrhic victory," said the General.

（10）Unemployment, like the sword of Damocles, was always accompanying the workers.

Exercises for Students（练习题）

Translate the following sentences into Chinese.

（1）The genius, wit, and spirit of a nation are discovered in its proverbs.

（2）Learning makes a good man better and an ill man worse.

（3）The wedding ring is worn on the ring finger of the left hand. People believe that a vein from the third finger runs directly to the heart.

（4）He that is truly wise and great, lives both too early and too late．

（5）*The Tempest* was Shakespeare's swan song in 1612.

（6）With determination, with luck, and with the help from lots of good people, I was able to rise from the ashes.

（7）What he said was true and had a leg to stand on.

（8）She has all her eggs in one basket with this merger deal. If it doesn't work out, I doubt her company can survive.

（9）John is always lazed and was all mouth and trousers before others.

（10）Several factors combined to depress the American economy.

（11）The boy looks very naughty, but he has his nose in a book.

7.2 Techniques of Translating English into Chinese on Difference in Cultural Consciousness（文化意识差异的英译汉技巧）

翻译是两个语言社区（language community）之间的交际过程和交际工具。王佐良先生说过："翻译里最大困难是什么呢？就是两种文化的不同。在一种文化里有一些不言而喻的东西，在另外一种文化里却要花很大力气加以解释。"

翻译在文化交流中起着非常重要的作用。由于不同的文化之间差异很大，在翻译过程中要弄清文化背景，正确理解原文，正确处理其中涉及的这些文化因素，认识语言的本质，把握其中的客观规律，熟悉文化异同，才能做好翻译的工作。汉译时，处理文化差异的几种常用方法有直译法、意译法、译文加注法（增补译法）等。

1. 直译法

直译法是一种比较常用的翻译方法，主要是在保留原文意思的基础上，尽量把原文的特点传递至译文中，最大程度还原原文的背景和文化色彩。尤其在英语典故的翻译中，要在理解原文的基础上，尽可能呈现典故的含义。例如：

Feed a cold and starve a fever.（伤风时宜吃，发热时宜饿。）

Every rose has its thorn.（没有无刺的玫瑰。）

Every rule has its exceptions.（任何规则都有例外。）

Failure is the mother of success.（失败是成功之母。）

Fight fire with fire.（以火攻火。）

Fools will be fools.（傻瓜总是傻瓜。）

Forbidden fruit is sweet.（禁果最甜。）

Habit is second nature.（习惯成自然。）

Strike while the iron is hot.（趁热打铁。）

Practice makes perfect.（熟能生巧。）

Example is better than precept.（身教胜于言传。）

Spend money like water.（挥金如土。）

All roads lead to Rome.（条条大路通罗马。）

a stick and carrot policy（大棒加胡萝卜政策）

Blood is thicker than water.（血浓于水。）

Versions for Appreciation（译文赏析）

（1）Put all of these codes on a paper, so you won't have to rack your brain to remember them anymore.

【译文】 把这些密码都写在一张纸上，你就不用绞尽脑汁去记了。

【评析】 "rack"有"剥削、榨取、使痛苦"的意思，"rack your brain"直译就是"剥削、榨取你的大脑，使之痛苦"，和汉语"绞尽脑汁"契合。

（2）I'm not going to tell you the secret because you have a big mouth.

【译文】 我不会把秘密告诉你，因为你是个大嘴巴。

【评析】 英语的"big mouth"和汉语的"大嘴巴"在意义上是接近的，都有"口风不紧，容易泄露消息"的意思，因而直译即可。

（3）The mayor made John treasurer; that's setting the fox to keep the geese.

【译文】 市长任命约翰当司库，这简直是叫狐狸看守鹅群。

【评析】 如果我们采用意译,"市长任命约翰当司库,简直是引狼入室。"这样的译文表面读起来很顺,可译文却改变了原文的比喻形象,抹去了原文的异国情调,因而直译更佳。

(4) He walked at the head of the funeral procession, and every now and then wiped away his crocodile tears with a big handkerchief.

【译文】 他走在送葬队伍的前头,还不时用一条大手绢抹去他那鳄鱼的眼泪。

【评析】 译文把原文作者的修辞所要达到的效果,即"猫哭老鼠",体现得淋漓尽致。虽然在汉语中本没有这种表达,但是由于直译可以保留原文生动形象的比喻,因此采取直译。

(5) A teacher tells us "hear much, speak little" everywhere we work.

【译文】 老师告诉我们无论在哪里工作,都要多听少说。

【评析】 句中的"hear much, speak little"是个英语谚语。本句采用直译方法。

(6) Bill said slowly, "He know you. You would rather to reign in hell, than serve in heaven."

【译文】 比尔先生慢慢地说道:"他了解你。你是宁为地狱王,不做天堂臣的。"

【评析】 假如此句意译为"宁为鸡首,不为牛尾",其内容信息似乎没有损失,但是,原文所表现出来的那种浓厚的宗教色彩却消失殆尽,其独特的意味不复存在了。

2. 意译法

文化既有共性,也有个性。文化共性是语言交流的基础,文化个性容易引起语言交流障碍。文化个性反映到词汇里,便会出现"词汇空缺"和"词汇冲突"的现象,反映到语法里,便会出现语言结构上的差异。如果这种文化差异和语言形象不为译入语读者所熟悉和接受,且翻译时仅仅直译的话,必然会引起误会和不理解。这时候,就可以采用意译法,将其基本含义和表达色彩呈现给译文读者。例如:

Bad workmen often blamed their tools.(拙匠常怪工具差。)

have an oar in everyman's boat （多管闲事）

第 7 章 Cultural Consciousness in English-Chinese Translation（英译汉中的文化意识）

bread buttered on both sides　（安适的境遇）

shoot the breeze　（吹牛/说大话）

As you brew, so you must drink.　（自作自受/自食其果）

make buckle and tongue meet　（量入为出/收支相抵）

a drop in the bucket　（沧海一粟）

Mind your own business.　（不要你管。）

Business is business.　（公事公办）

You cannot eat your cake and have it.　（两者不可兼得。）

kill the fatted calf　（设宴欢迎）

call a spade a spade　（是啥说啥/直言不讳）

not worth the candle　（得不偿失）

Versions for Appreciation（译文赏析）

（1）He is a man of family.

【译文】　他出身名门。

【评析】　这句话如果按照字面意义翻成"他是一个有家室的人。"就是没有领会英语文化中"of family"出自名门的意思，因此在涉及文化差异的场景下，有时候需要采用意译才能将相关信息准确地翻译出来。

（2）Insecurity, unemployment and the "rat race" of the American life place heavy strains on marriage and the family.

【译文】　失业和缺乏保障以及美国生活的激烈竞争给婚姻和家庭带来了沉重的压力。

【评析】　"rat race"在英语里是"激烈竞争""争权夺利"的意思，如果按字面意思译成"老鼠赛跑"就无法将文化含义准确地翻译出来，因此只能意译。

（3）Heaven never helps the man who will not act.

【译文】　天不助懒人。

【评析】　这句话是一个谚语。如果将此句译为"天从不帮助没有行动的人",寓意表达不明,只有采用意译的方法,表意才简洁明了。

(4) The president showed unexpected strength, especially in the wet districts.

【译文】 这位总统出其不意地得到了很多选票,尤其在非禁酒地区。

【评析】 句中的关键处有二:一是"showed unexpected strength"不能直译为"显示出出乎意料的力量",这是西方国家竞选时常使用的语言,为"出其不意地得到选票"之意;二是"wet districts"不能直译为"潮湿地区",而是"非禁酒区"。

(5) Happy is the bride the sun shines on.

【译文】 吉日宜结婚。

【评析】 这句话是一个谚语。如果将此句译为"太阳出来了,新娘高兴"就是误译,而且也不知所云。所以只能采取意译。

(6) The next week was family conference, something I dreaded, which was the day the dirty laundry got hung out to air in a private session between parent, child and counselor.

【译文】 下周将开家长会,这正是我害怕的。在这一天,家长、孩子和辅导员将开私下的碰头会,列数孩子做的坏事。

【评析】 原文中"the dirty laundry got hung out to air"比喻形象,但直译效果并不是很好,因此使用变通的方法对译文中比喻形象的流失做一些补偿,译为"家长、孩子和辅导员将开私下的碰头会,列数孩子做的坏事",不仅传达出了隐含的喻义,而且还保留了原文幽默风趣的语气,是一个好的译文。

3. 译文加注法 / 增补译法

英汉民族文化背景不同。因为英语中某些文化词语在汉语中根本就没有对等词,形成了词义上的空缺,所以英译汉时常常要采用加注法来弥补空缺。加注法或增补法通常用来补充诸如背景材料、词语起源等相关信息,便于读者理解。使用译文加注法或增补译法,即对原文先直译后再加注的方法,既保持译文与原文"意"相似,又能做到准确理解其文化现象。

(1) Bill had been faithful to the vicar's daughter whom he had

第 7 章 Cultural Consciousness in English-Chinese Translation（英译汉中的文化意识）

worshipped on his knees but had never led to the altar.

【译文】 比尔一直忠于牧师的女儿。他曾经拜倒在她的石榴裙下，但却没有和她走进结婚的殿堂。

【评析】 如按照字面意思，逐字逐句翻译原文，会使汉语译文的读者不知所云。此处采用"形存意释"的方法，将"had never led to the altar"译为"却没有和她走进结婚的殿堂"，形象和意义都得到了保留，体现了原文的修辞风格和表达效果。

（2）Let both sides unite to heed in all corners of the earth the command of Isaiah to "undo the heavy burdens ... (and) let the oppressed go free".

【译文】 不管我们在地球的什么地方，让我们双方都记住基督教先知以赛亚的重托："卸下重负……让所有受压迫的人都获得自由"。

【评析】 该句是肯尼迪在简短的就职演说中的一句。据《旧约》记载，以赛亚是位先知，他富有教养、才华超众、不畏权势、预言以色列总有一天会得救。演讲中提到这个名字，对信奉基督教的西方人来讲，其号召力和寓意是不言而喻的。但是，若直接将"Isaiah"译为"以赛亚"，不加任何解释说明，不说其联想意义，很多中国读者甚至不知其为何许人也。所以此处必须使用增补译法。

（3）Like a son of Bacchus, he can drink up two bottles of whisky at a breath.

【译文】 他简直像酒神巴克斯的儿子，能一口气喝光两瓶威士忌。

【评析】 "Bacchus"是古希腊神话中的酒神，音译为"巴克斯"，这对不熟悉西方文化的读者来说不好理解，加注"酒神"就很好地解决了这个问题。

（4）He saw himself, in a smart suit, bowed into the opulent suites of Ritzes.

【译文】 他发现自己身着漂亮的礼服，被恭恭敬敬地引进了像里兹饭店一般豪华的旅馆客房里下榻。

【评析】 "Ritzes"指的是"里兹饭店"，原为瑞士人里兹开设，以豪华著称。在翻译时增补"饭店"就能使读者一下子看懂这句话的含义，避免他们不知道里兹是一家豪华饭店而无法读懂句义。

（5）But I am short-tempered, frazzled from all responsibilities. I am the "sandwich generation".

【译文】 但我的脾气不好，都是这些事给烦的。我是个夹在孩子和父母之间的"三明治人"。

【评析】 译文基本采用直译，在最后一句中采用了译文加注的方法增补了"夹在孩子和父母之间的"，以免中国读者因为不明白"三明治"的含义而产生误解。

Questions for Teacher's Lecture（讲解题）

Translate the following sentences into Chinese.

（1）It is unfair that some historians always attribute the fall of kingdoms to Helen of Troy.

（2）His mother always looked the other way when he was naughty.

（3）She scolded her maid and was as cross as two sticks.

（4）But it's as dark as Egypt outdoors. We might go tomorrow if there's a moon.

（5）People considered that what he had played on that occasion was no more than a Judas kiss.

（6）South African leopard spot came under the fierce black fire.

（7）I think you should choose the lesser of two evils.

（8）Fine feathers make fine birds.

Exercises for Students（练习题）

Translate the following sentences into Chinese.

（1）Can the Leopard change his spots?

（2）The doctors tell us it's dangerous to smoke, but such good advice rolls off some people like water off a duck's back.

（3）Bill's new girlfriend is certainly a knockout.

（4）I am as poor as Job, my lord, but not so patient.

（5）Everybody made suggestion, but no one actually offered to bell the cat.

（6）The man who waters his grass after a good rain is carrying coals to Newcastle.

第 8 章

Translation of Discourse
（语篇翻译）

语篇（discourse）是一系列句子构成的语言整体。对篇章的理解不能断章取义，只见树木不见森林，要先弄清文章主题，再对词句进行微观分析，篇中求句，句中求字。决定语篇语言应用特征的首要因素就是文体。不同的文体对语言表达的方式要求也不尽相同。例如：文学类语篇偏重语言的创造性、形象性、象征性，而科技类语篇强调表述客观、逻辑严密、行文规范、用词和句式准确等。语篇的文体是翻译中要着重考虑的因素。以下面一语段的翻译为例。

China is right in the accelerating course of urbanization, which, nevertheless, will pose two possibilities at the critical moment. On the one hand, the healthy development of urbanization will form the mainstream trend to boost the sustained economic growth and the overall social progress; on the other hand, the downside of the double-edged sword will entail inability to lead failure in governmental policy, deterioration of the issues of agriculture, farmers, and the countryside, which in turn will accelerate the polarization of township and countryside, over dependence of growth on investment, low ratio of tertiary industry in the economy, heavy pressure on the resource distribution, as well as inadequate supply of skilled labors, etc.

【译文】 我国正处于城市化加速发展的阶段。但也处于存在两种可能的重要关口。一种可能是城市化健康发展，成为带动经济持续增长和社会全面进步的主流趋势；另一种可能是引导不力、政策失当，出现偏差，带来"三农"问题加剧、城乡两极分化、增长继续过于依赖投资、服务业比重难以提高、资源大跨度调动压力加大、高素质劳动力供给不足等问题。

【评析】 这是一篇政论性语篇的片段，叙述逻辑性强，客观地反映事实情况，行文规范，用词和句式准确，结构紧密。

8.1 Translation of Literary Writings（文学语篇翻译）

文学类作品的语言与实用文体的语言有不同的特点。文学作品是来自生活又高于生活的艺术作品,它有艺术的语言,有审美价值,其语篇功能主要是用艺术的语言叙事、画物、言情,以达到感染人、愉悦人、教育人的目的。文学语言是最讲求音韵、节奏、意境的语言。文学体裁可分为三大类,即叙事类、抒情类、戏剧类。根据文学作品在意象建构、体裁结构、语言运用、表现方法等方面的不同,又可将其分为散文、小说、诗歌、戏剧文学等。

1. 散文的翻译

散文包括抒情散文、游记、日记、报告文学、随笔、杂文、传记、小品文等,其特点是篇幅短小、结构自由、富有诗意、手法多样,可以抒情,也可叙事和议论,极为自由。散文语言清新自然、活泼灵秀、洗练畅达,能带给人美感。

散文的翻译不能机械地直译,否则散文的"形"与"神"将难以统一。散文的韵味一般体现在三点:声音和节奏,意境和氛围,以及作家独特的语言风格。要想译散文需要译者不断锤炼自己的语言功底并不断增强自己的艺术鉴赏力。

Versions for Appreciation(译文赏析)

(1) It was a day as fresh as grass growing up and clouds going over and butterflies coming down can make it. It was a day compounded from silences of bee and flower and ocean and land, which were not silences at all, but motions, stirs, flutters, risings, fallings, each in its own time and matchless rhythm.

【译文】 绿草萋萋,白云冉冉,彩蝶翩翩,这日子是如此清新;蜜蜂无言,春花不语,海波声歇,大地音寂,这日子是如此安静。然而并非安静,因为万物各以其独特的节奏,或动,或摇,或震,或起,或伏。

【评析】 原文是一段描写春天的句子,叙述有条不紊,采用了两个排比句"it was a day"。由于排比句的使用,作者可以做到一抒胸臆,从容洒脱,同时在第二句中为表示与安静相对的意思,使用了一系列具有强烈动词意味的名词"motions""stirs""flutters""risings""fallings"。该句翻译堪称佳译。首先，作者保留了原文的两个排比句，用了"这日子是如此清新"和"这日子是如此安静"。其次，原文中的"motions""stirs""flutters""risings""fallings"译者用了"或动，或摇，或震，或起，或伏"平行结构来译，同时，发挥了汉语动词丰富的优势。另外，译文当中"萋萋""冉冉""翩翩"三个叠音词所传达出的一种意境之美，只要是以汉语为母语的读者，都可感悟其妙处。

（2）Wives have been killed, babies born deformed, husbands left deserted, children crippled in accidents, homes burned to the ground—I have looked and heard and wept and thought this is too much for anyone to bear... and then I have been astounded at how happiness of a kind can be regained out of the hell of grief.

【译文】 妻子被杀，婴儿畸形，丈夫被弃，儿童致残，房屋焚毁——我目睹，我耳闻，我哭泣，我想：如此灾难，在这个世上，何人能承受！……然而接下去，我之所见，让我震惊，人们如何一步步走出悲恸的地狱，获得了这样那样的幸福。

【评析】 原文写得激情澎湃，扣人心弦，这种效果与短句的平行使用和单词的平行使用不无关系，在选词上，运用最直接、最简单的表达宣泄作者的感情。译文基本采用直译，首先将第一句中的短句平行结构移植到译文中，采用了汉语常用的四字结构，"妻子被杀，婴儿畸形，丈夫被弃，儿童致残，房屋焚毁"。为了达到这种一气呵成的效果，译者在处理"children crippled in accidents""homes burned to the ground"两句时，采用了减词法，在接下来的三个单词平行结构上，作者采用了重复法，"我目睹，我耳闻，我哭泣，我想"，重复主语"我"，此处增词、减词的使用，使译文更适合中文读者的口味。在最后一句的处理上，译者采用了拆分译法，将英语结构严谨的长句拆分成汉语习惯的松散句，更贴近译语读者的理解模式。此译文可谓形神兼备。

（3）The first drops of rain are huge. They splat into the dust and imprint the windows with individual signatures. They plink on the vent pipe and plunk on the patio roof. Leaves shudder under their weight before rebounding, and the sidewalk wears a coat of shiny spots.

【译文】 最初的雨点大粒大粒的，扑扑地打在尘土里，在窗玻璃上留下一个个印记。雨点把排气管敲得叮叮当当，把院子顶棚打得噼噼啪啪。树叶被砸得瑟瑟发抖，难以抬头。人行道披上了一层亮晶晶的水珠。

【评析】 这段文字选自一篇描写暴风雨的美文。这段文字中三个拟声词"splat""plink""plunk"的运用鲜活有力。拟声词是按照某种语言的语音系统对客观世界的声音加以模拟改造的结果，所以不可避免地带有该语言的发音特征。翻译英语拟声词时，除了闻声解意外，还应考虑具体语境和修辞等要求。译文中拟声叠音词"扑扑地""叮叮当当""噼噼啪啪""瑟瑟发抖"的出现，使原文的音韵美得到了理想演绎。

（4）An individual human existence should be like a river—small at first, narrowly contained within its banks, and rushing passionately past boulders and over waterfalls. Gradually the river grows wider, the banks recede, the waters flow more quietly, and in the end, without any visible break, they become merged in the sea, and painlessly lose their individual being.

【译文】 个人的存在应像河流，起初是涓涓细流，夹在窄窄的两岸之间，接着热情澎湃地冲过巨石，飞下瀑布。渐渐地，河面变宽，两岸离得越来越远，河流逐渐平缓，最后绵延不断地汇入大海，毫无痛苦地失去自我的存在。

【评析】 原文将人的一生比作河流，用这种巧妙的比喻将原本看不见摸不着的生命状态生动形象地呈现在读者面前。字里行间充满智慧，思辨性强，读来朗朗上口。同样，译文也体现了这些特点。用"冲过""飞下""汇入"等一系列动感十足的词汇来描绘河流从发源到最终奔腾入海的画面，其中"涓涓细流""热情澎湃""绵延不绝"等词语更是锦上添花，原本就生动活泼的画面经过译者的三言两笔立体感愈加强烈。而最后"毫无痛苦"一词宛如神来之笔，因为河流本无痛感可言，这一笔便将河流的生命感体现到极致。此时，读者已分不清面前的是一条河流还是一位暮色垂垂的老者。而这一点，正是原文作者想要达到的效果，原文的比喻是成功的，译文也毫不逊色。

Questions for Teacher's Lecture（讲解题）

Translate the following essays into Chinese.

（1）The winding course of the stream continually shut out the scene behind us and revealed as calm and lovely a one before. We glided from depth to depth, and breathed new seclusion at every turn. The shy kingfisher flew from the withered branch close at hand to another at distance, uttering a shrill cry of anger or alarm. Ducks that had been floating there since the preceding eve were startled at our approach and skimmed along the glassy river, breaking its dark surface with a bright streak. The pickerel leaped from among the lily pads. The turtle, sunning itself upon a rock or at the root of a tree, slid suddenly into the water with a plunge. The painted Indian who paddled his canoe along the Assabeth three hundred years ago could hardly have seen a wilder gentleness displayed upon its banks and reflected in its bosom than we did. Nor could the same Indian have prepared his noontide meal with more simplicity. We drew up our skiff at some point where the overarching shade formed a natural bower, and there kindled a fire with the pine cones and decayed branches that lay strewn plentifully around.

（2）I went to the woods because I wished to live deliberately, to front only the essential facts of life, and see if I could not learn what it had to teach, and not, when I came to die, discover that I had not lived. I did not wish to live what was not life, living is so dear; nor did I wish to practice resignation, unless it was quite necessary. I wanted to live deep and suck out all the marrow of life, to live so sturdily and Spartan-like as to put to rout all that was not life, to cut a broad swath and shave close, to drive life into a corner, and reduce it to its lowest terms, and, if it proved to be mean, why then to get the whole and genuine meanness of it, and publish its meanness to the word; or if it were sublime, to know it by experience, and be able to give a true account of it in my next excursion.

Still we live meanly, like ants; though the fable tells us that we were long ago changed into men; like pygmies we fight with cranes; it is error upon error, and clout upon clout, and our best virtue has for its occasion a superfluous and evitable wretchedness. Our life is frittered away by detail. An honest man has hardly needed to count more than his ten fingers, or in extreme cases he may add his ten toes, and lump the rest. Simplicity, simplicity,

Exercises for Students(练习题)

Translate the following essay into Chinese.

There are a great many people who have all the material conditions of happiness, i.e. health and a sufficient income, and who, nevertheless, are profoundly unhappy. In such cases it would seem as if the fault must lie with a wrong theory as to how to live. In one sense, we may say that any theory as to how to live is wrong. We imagine ourselves more different from the animals than we are. Animals live on impulse, and are happy as long as external conditions are favorable. If you have a cat it will enjoy life if it has food and warmth and opportunities for an occasional night on the titles. Your needs are more complex than those of your cat, but they still have their basis in instinct. In civilized societies, this is too apt to be forgotten. People propose to themselves some one paramount objective, and restrain all impulses that do not minister to it. A businessman may be so anxious to grow rich that to this end he sacrifices health and private affections. When at last he has become rich, no pleasure remains to him except harrying other people by exhortations to imitate his noble example. Many rich ladies, although nature has endowed them with any spontaneous pleasure in literature or art, decide to be thought cultured, and spend boring hours learning the right thing to say about fashionable new books that are written to give delight, not to afford opportunities for dusty snobbish.

If you look around at the men and women whom you can call happy, you will see that they all have certain things in common. The most important of these things is an activity which at most gradually builds up something that you are glad to see coming into existence. Women who take an instinctive pleasure in their children can get this kind of satisfaction out of bringing up a family. Artists and authors and men of science get happiness in this way if their own work seems good to them. But there are many humbler forms of the same kind of pleasure. Many men who spend their working life in the city devote their weekends to voluntary and unremunerated toil in their gardens, and when the spring comes, they experience all the joys of having created beauty.

The whole subject of happiness has, in my opinion, been treated too solemnly. It had been thought that man cannot be happy without a theory of life or a religion. Perhaps those who have been rendered unhappy by a bad theory may need a better theory to help them to recovery, just as you may need a tonic when you have been ill. But when things are normal a man should be healthy without a tonic and happy without a theory. It is the simple things that really matter. If a man delights in his wife and children, has success in work, and finds pleasure in the alternation of day and night, spring and autumn, he will be happy whatever his philosophy may be. If, on the other hand, he finds his wife fateful, his children's noise unendurable, and the office a nightmare; if in the daytime he longs for night, and at night sighs for the light of day, then what he needs is not a new philosophy but a new regimen—a different diet, or more exercise, or what not.

2. 小说的翻译

小说是一种通过故事情节的叙述来塑造人物、反映社会生活的文学体裁。它细致且多方面地刻画人物性格，生动且完整地叙述故事情节,充分地、多方面地展现人物活动的环境。小说与画和音乐不同,它以语言文字为媒介,描绘自然景观、社会环境、人物言谈举止、心理变化。

小说虽然题材各异,但都离不开人物、情节、语言、风格这些创作要素。译者需注意以下问题:

第一,文字要准确精练,所译人物形象要切合人物特点。塑造形象是小说的主要任务。小说通过艺术形象来影响读者,特别注意用词的精练。所以,翻译时译者必须细心地体味原文含意,揣度人物的形象、个性,然后选用确切的词语,将人物栩栩如生地表达出来。

第二,译者不可对人物等表现出主观的倾向性。译者首先是读者,必然会被原作感染,但是在翻译过程中,译者不可以将自己的个人好恶作为标准,将这种感情倾向性在译作中体现出来。但如果是作者对小说中的主人公有好感,字里行间都流露出对他的赞美,这种倾向性就需要通过译入语文字传达给目的语读者了。

第三,译事要合乎情理和事理。翻译原作者对情节、事件的叙述时,要合情合理,不能自相矛盾,不能出现无法自圆其说的语句,不能出现前后失去照应的情况。

第四,译情译景要逼真,要使人有身临其境之感。对于原文艺术形象的情态,译者不能有一丝一毫的疏忽,必须把人物的喜怒哀乐表现出来。

总之,小说中的语言是塑造形象、刻画性格的重要手段。翻译小说,必须将人物的出身、社会地位、职业、文化、经历、环境特点体现出来。

Versions for Appreciation(译文赏析)

(1) Mrs. Bennet was in fact too much overpowered to say a great deal while Sir William remained; but no sooner had he left them than her feelings found a rapid vent. In the first place, she persisted in disbelieving the whole of the matter; secondly, she was very sure that Mr. Collins had been taken in;

thirdly, she trusted that they wouldn't ever be happy together; and fourthly, that the match might be broken off. Two inferences, however, were plainly deduced from the whole; one, that Elizabeth was the real cause of all the mischief, and the other, that she herself had been barbarously used by them all; and on these two points she principally dwelt during the rest of the day. Nothing could console and nothing appease her.

【译文】 班纳特太太在威廉爵士面前，实在气得说不出话。可是他一走，她那一肚子牢骚便马上发泄出来。第一，她坚决不相信这回事；第二，她断定柯林斯先生受了骗；第三，她相信这一对夫妇决不会幸福；第四，这门亲事可能会破裂。不过，她却从整个事件上简单地得出了两个结论——一个是这场笑话全都是伊丽莎白一手造成的，另一个是她自己受尽了大家的欺侮虐待；在那一整天里，她所谈的大都是这两点。怎么也安慰不了她，怎么也平不了她的气。

【评析】 在 *Pride and Prejudice*（《傲慢与偏见》）中，因为家产的关系，班纳特太太一心想要远房侄子柯林斯先生娶女儿伊丽莎白为妻，但伊丽莎白却断然拒绝了柯林斯的求婚。柯林斯转而与夏洛特订了婚，班纳特太太则完全被蒙在鼓里。因此，当威廉爵士登门通报女儿与柯林斯订婚的消息时，就出现了上面这一幕。在读这一段时，我们可以明显地感受到一种反讽的效果。这一效果主要来自"in the first place""secondly""thirdly"等顺序词所带来的表面上的逻辑性与实际上的逻辑混乱——"she persisted in disbelieving the whole of the matter""was very sure that Mr. Collins had been taken in"——之间形成的强烈反差。这些顺序词通过对照、反差讽刺性地突出了班纳特太太话语的自相矛盾之处。原文中的"Two inferences, however, were plainly deduced from the whole..."这一表达方式具有较强的学术味，它与推论本身的庸俗气形成了鲜明对照，使人更感到班纳特太太俗不可耐，这是作者暗地嘲讽人物的绝妙手法。译文中，译者用"第一""第二""第三""第四"等顺序词以及"坚持不相信""断定""相信"等词语将原作中表面上的逻辑性与实际上的逻辑混乱之间形成的鲜明对照保留下来，同样具有强烈的反讽效果。

（2）Eisenhower later recalled, when MacArthur felt slighted he was capable of expressing himself in "an explosive denunciation of politics, bad manners, bad judgment, broken promise, arrogance, unconstitutionality, insensitivity, and the way the world had gone to hell."

【译文】 艾森豪威尔后来回忆往事时说，只要麦克阿瑟感到有人对他不够尊重，就"发起脾气来，破口大骂人家好耍权术，不懂礼貌，乱出主意，出尔反尔，狂妄自大，违反宪法，神经迟钝，麻木不仁，如今世道真是见鬼。"

【评析】 这句话选自威廉·曼彻斯特的《光荣与梦想》，译文中连续出现了八个四字格。总体来说，汉语中的四字格一共有两大类，一类是汉语成语的四字格，另一类是由普通词语构成的四字格。四字格有三大优点：言简意赅、整齐对称和读来朗朗上口。译文中"出尔反尔""狂妄自大"和"麻木不仁"均属于汉语成语，而其他几个则是由普通词语组成的四字格。这八个四字格如同密集的雨点一般对麦克阿瑟进行了连续且强有力的批判，人物形象一下跃然纸上。译文既做到了忠实于原文，又显得异常生动，有效地传递了原文的意义。

（3）"Madam, after her six years' residence at the Mall, I have the honor and happiness of presenting Miss Amelia Sedley to her parents, as young lady not unworthy to occupy a fitting position in their polished and refined circle. Those virtues which characterize the young English gentlewoman, those accomplishments which become her birth and station, will not be found wanting in the amiable Miss Sedley, whose industry and obedience have endeared her to her instructors, and whose delightful sweetness of temper has charmed her aged and her youthful companions."

【译文】 "夫人，爱米丽亚·塞特丽小姐在林荫道女校生活六年之后，我万分荣幸并欢欣地将她奉还府上。在他们这样有教养的氛围中，作为一位年轻的贵族小姐，她安全可以占有一席相宜之地位。那些英国大家闺秀拥有的美德，那些与身世相称的才学在爱米丽娅·塞特丽身上无有缺憾，她的勤勉和恭顺博得师长钟爱，她那可人的温和气质倍受长幼一致赞赏。"

【评析】 这是 *Vanity Fair*（《名利场》）中平克顿小姐给爱米丽亚母亲的信，这封信矫饰冗赘，阿谀奉承，故作高雅风格，原文用了一系列"大词"，如 "present" "virtues" "want" "endear" 等，以及众多的褒义形容词。在句法上，则用了相对正式的文体，并采用平行结构增强语势。译文用了"奉还""府上"等表示说话人语气谦卑的词，同时还使用了一些汉语擅长的四字形容词词组，如"万分荣幸""风雅高尚"。此外，一些具有文言色彩的词也传递出说话人奉承的口气，如"相宜之地位"，同时保留了双重否定语 "not unworthy to occupy"（完全可以），强化了平克顿小姐咬文嚼字，阿谀奉承的伪态，从而更完整地再现了原著风格。

(4) I have not been trampled on. I have not been petrified. I have not been buried with inferior minds, and excluded from every glimpse of communion with what is bright and energetic and high.

【译文】 我未曾遭人践踏，未曾变得麻木，未曾埋没于小人堆里，在品味一切明媚灿烂，生机勃勃和高尚脱俗之事时我也未曾受到排斥。

【评析】 本段选自夏洛特·勃朗特的 *Jane Eyre*（《简·爱》），这是简·爱得知罗切斯特先生要结婚，以为自己要永远离开桑菲尔德后发自肺腑的感伤之言。这部分共有三个句子，简·爱借此介绍了自己在桑菲尔德的快乐生活，回顾了自己来到桑菲尔德，认识罗切斯特先生的美好，表达了深深的不舍。三句话表达的含义是一气呵成的，因此翻译时，使用"未曾……未曾……未曾……也未曾……"这样的排比结构将其处理为一个完整的句子，更能突出简·爱此刻无法抑制的情感。而译文中"遭人践踏""变得麻木""明媚灿烂""生机勃勃"和"高尚脱俗"五个四字格，言简意赅，将原文中字里行间简·爱对罗切斯特的尊敬和爱戴体现得淋漓尽致。

Questions for Teacher's Lecture（讲解题）

Translate the following passages into Chinese.

(1) There is an ecstasy that marks the summit of life, and beyond

which life cannot rise. And such is the paradox of living, this ecstasy comes when one is most alive, and it comes as a complete forgetfulness that one is alive. This ecstasy, this forgetfulness of living, comes to the artist, caught up and out of himself in a sheet of flame; it comes to the soldier, war-mad on a stricken field and refusing quarter; and it came to Buck, leading the pack, sounding the old wolf-cry, straining after the food that was alive and that fled swiftly before him through the moonlight. He was sounding the deeps of his nature, and of the parts of his nature that were deeper than he, going back into the womb of Time. He was mastered by the sheer surging of life, the tidal wave of being, the perfect joy of each separate muscle, joint, and sinew in that it was everything that was not death, that it was aglow and rampant, expressing itself in movement, flying exultantly under the stars and over the face of dead matter that did not move.

But Spitz, cold and calculating even in his supreme moods, left the pack and cut across a narrow neck of land where the creek made a long bend around. Buck did not know of this, and as he rounded the bend, the frost wraith of a rabbit still fitting before him, he saw another and larger frost wraith leap from the overhanging bank into the immediate path of the rabbit. It was Spitz. The rabbit could not turn, and as the white teeth broke its back in mid air it shrieked as loudly as a stricken man may shriek. At sound of this, the cry of Life plunging down from Life's apex in the grip of Death, the fall pack at Buck's heels raised a hell's chorus of delight.

Buck did not cry out. He did not check himself, but drove in upon Spitz, shoulder to shoulder, so hard that he missed the throat. They rolled over and over in the powdery snow. Spitz gained his feet almost as though he had not been overthrown, slashing Buck down the shoulder and leaping clear. Twice his teeth clipped together, like the steel jaws of a trap, as he backed away for better footing, with lean and lifting lips that writhed and snarled.

（2）Along this same footpath, Oliver well-remembered he had trotted beside Mr. Bumble, when he first carried him to the workhouse from the farm. His way lay directly in front of the cottage. His heart beat quickly when he bethought himself of this; and he half resolved to turn back. He had come a long way though, and should lose a great deal of time by doing so. Besides, it was so early that there was very little fear of his being seen; so he walked on.

He reached the house. There was no appearance of its inmates stirring at that early hour. Oliver stopped, and peeped into the garden. A child was weeding one of the little beds; as he stopped, he raised his pale face and disclosed the features of one of his former companions. Oliver felt glad to see him, before he went; for, though younger than himself, he had been his little friend and playmate. They had been beaten, and starved, and shut up together, many and many a time.

"Hush, Dick!" said Oliver, as the boy ran to the gate, and thrust his thin arm between the rails to greet him. "Is any one up?"

"Nobody but me," replied the child.

"You mustn't say you saw me, Dick," said Oliver. "I am running away. They beat and ill-use me, Dick; and I am going to seek my fortune, some long way off. I don't know where. How pale you are!"

"I heard the doctor tell them I was dying," replied the child with a faint smile. "I am very glad to see you, dear; but don't stop, don't stop!"

"Yes, yes, I will, to say good-bye to you," replied Oliver. "I shall see you again, Dick. I know I shall! You will be well and happy!"

"I hope so," replied the child. "After I am dead, but not before. I know the doctor must be right, Oliver, because I dream so much of Heaven, and Angels, and kind faces that I never see when I am awake. Kiss me," said the child, climbing up the low gate, and flinging his little arms round Oliver's neck. "Good-by, dear! God bless you!"

The blessing was from a young child's lips, but it was the first that Oliver had ever heard invoked upon his head; and through the struggles and sufferings, and troubles and changes, of his after life, he never once forgot it.

Exercises for Students(练习题)

Translate the following passage into Chinese.

Gabriel Oak was a sensible man of good character, who had been brought up by his father as a shepherd, and then managed to save enough money to rent his own farm on Norcombe Hill, in Dorset. He was twenty-eight, a tall well-built man, who did not seem, however, to think his appearance was very important.

One winter morning he was in one of his fields on the side of Norcombe Hill. Looking over his gate, Gabriel could see a yellow cart, loaded with furniture and plants, coming up the road. Right on top of the pile sat a handsome young woman. As Gabriel was watching, the cart stopped at the top of the hill, and the driver climbed down to go back and fetch something that had fallen off.

The girl sat quietly in the sunshine for a few minutes. Then she picked up a parcel lying next to her, and looked round to see if the driver was coming back. There was no sign of him. She unwrapped the parcel, and took out the mirror it contained. The sun shone on her lovely face and hair. Although it was December, she looked almost summery, sitting there in her bright red jacket with the fresh green plants around her. She looked at herself in the mirror and smiled, thinking that only the birds could see her. But behind the gate Gabriel Oak was watching too. "She must be rather vain," he thought, "She doesn't need to look in that mirror at all!"

As the girl smiled and blushed at herself, she seemed to be dreaming, dreaming perhaps of men's hearts won and lost. When she heard the driver's footsteps, she packed the mirror away. The cart moved on downhill to the tollgate. Gabriel followed on foot. As he came closer he could hear the driver arguing with the gatekeeper.

"My mistress's niece, that's her on top of the furniture, is not going to pay you the extra two pence," said the driver. "She says she's offered you quite enough already." "Well, if she doesn't pay the toll, your mistress'niece can't pass through the gate," replied the gatekeeper. Gabriel thought that two pence did not seem worth bothering about, so he stepped forward. "Here," he said, handing the coins to the gatekeeper, "let the young woman pass."

The girl in the red jacket looked carelessly down at Gabriel, and told her man to drive on, without even thanking the farmer. Gabriel and the gatekeeper watched the cart move away. "That's a lovely young woman," said the gatekeeper. "But she has her faults," answered Gabriel.

"True, farmer." "And the greatest of them is what it always is with women." "Wanting to win the argument every time? Oh, you're right."

"No, her great fault is that she's vain."

A few days later, at nearly midnight on the longest night of the year, Gabriel Oak could be heard playing his flute on Norcombe Hill. The sky was so clear and the stars so visible that the earth could almost be seen turning. In that cold, hard air the sweet notes of the flute rang out. The music came from a little hut on wheels, standing in the corner of a field. Shepherds' huts like this are used as a shelter during the winter and spring, when shepherds have to stay out all night in the fields, looking after very young lambs.

Gabriel's two hundred and fifty sheep were not yet paid for. He knew that, in order to make a success of the farming business, he had to make sure they produced a large number of healthy lambs. So he was determined to spend as many nights as necessary in the fields, to save his lambs from dying of cold or hunger.

3. 诗歌的翻译

诗歌是用高度凝练的语言，形象地表达作者的丰富情感，集中反映社会生活并具有一定节奏和韵律的文学体裁。王佐良先生将英国史

第 8 章　Translation of Discourse（语篇翻译）

诗分为古英语时期、中古英语时期及近代英语时期。古英语诗歌中最重要的一部作品无疑要属长篇史诗 *Beowulf*（《贝奥武夫》），它是迄今为止发现的英国盎格鲁-撒克逊时期最古老、最长的一部较为完整的文学作品，也是欧洲最早的方言史诗，被誉为英国文学开山之作。英国湖畔诗人华兹华斯（William Wordsworth）认为"诗是强烈情感的自然流露"。爱尔兰诗人叶芝（William Butler Yeats）称"诗是心血、想象、智慧的交流"。诗歌作为一种高级的文学艺术形式，在语言上具有精练、形象、音调和谐、节奏鲜明等特点，在形式上不以句子为单位，而以行为单位，且分行主要根据节奏，而不以意思为准。

"形"与"神"是诗歌的重要构成因素。"形"是指诗歌的用词、句式、句法、修辞及表现手法等内容。而"神"，可以理解为诗歌中的意象及其延伸意义，以及诗作的神韵和精神。傅雷认为"翻译应当像临画一样，所求的不在形似而在神似"。因此，在翻译过程中，译者需充分了解原作者的写作背景和契机，以此把握诗歌所蕴含的情感及思想内容。诗歌本身具有音韵美、形式美和意象美的特点，其神韵也往往需要通过一定的形式来表现。神寓于形，形之不存，神将焉附？因此，重神似并不是完全抛开原诗的形式，而是以灵活的方式忠于原诗的音、形、意美。因此英诗翻译应该在恰如其分地传达原诗神韵的同时，尽可能地忠实于原诗的形式。试比较：

The days are in the yellow leaf,

The flowers and fruits of love are gone,

The worm, the canker, and the grief,

Are mine alone.

【译文 1】

年华黄叶秋，

花实空悠悠，

多情徒自苦，

残泪带愁留。

【译文 2】

我的岁月似深秋的黄叶，

爱情的香花甜果已凋残；
只有蛀虫、病毒和灾孽，
是我的财产！

细读以上译文可发现，前者在字数、韵律和平仄上都符合中国传统五言诗的形式特点，对仗工整，郎朗上口。但意象和写作风格都与拜伦的原诗相去甚远，晦涩难懂。而后者则是按照原诗的用词和形式来译，流畅自然，通俗易懂，在形式和内容上都与原诗高度统一。在内容上，译者以明喻代替暗喻，保留了原诗中的一切意象，适当增字以传达作者的情感；在形式上，译诗与原诗句式长短相当，用韵同为abab式，保留了原诗的"音美、形美、意美"。总之，译诗作为一种文学实践活动绝不是被动的，译者需主动进入原作的灵魂，进行有限制的"二次创作"，力求达到"神""形"兼备。

Versions for Appreciation（译文赏析）

（1）
The Road Not Taken
Robert Frost

Two roads diverged in a yellow wood,
And sorry I could not travel both
And be one traveler, long I stood
And looked down one as far as I could
To where it bent in the undergrowth.

Then took the other, as just as fair,
And having perhaps the better claim,
Because it was grassy and wanted wear;
Though as for that the passing there

Had worn them really about the same.

And both that morning equally lay
In leaves no step had trodden black.
Oh, I kept the first for another day!
Yet knowing how way leads on to way,
I doubted if I should ever come back.

I shall be telling this with a sigh
Somewhere ages and ages hence:
Two roads diverged in a wood, and I—
I took the one less traveled by,
And that has made all the difference.

【译文】
未选择的路
罗伯特·弗罗斯特

黄色的树林里分出两条路,
可惜我不能同时去涉足,
我在那路口久久伫立,
我向着一条路极目望去,
直到它消失在丛林深处。

但我却选了另外一条路,
它荒草萋萋,十分幽寂,
显得更诱人、更美丽,
虽然在这两条小路上,
都很少留下旅人的足迹,

虽然那天清晨落叶满地,

两条路都未经脚印污染。
呵，留下一条路等改日再见！
但我知道路径延绵无尽头，
恐怕我难以再回返。
也许多少年后在某个地方，

我将轻声叹息把往事回顾，
一片树林里分出两条路，
而我选了人迹更少的一条，
从此决定了我一生的道路。

【评析】 The Road Not Taken 这首诗共四节，每节五行，每行四个音步，每节韵脚均为 abaab，读起来整齐流畅，节奏感十足。诗歌的主要意象有二，其一为"traveler"——一个站在分岔路口无法抉择，踟蹰不前的旅人；其二则是"road"——两条无人问津、杂草丛生的路，这不单是寻常通行之路，更是象征了漫漫人生路。

译者将题目译作《未选择的路》，与原诗字字对应，通俗易懂。第一节前两句采用直译法，第三句省略了"and be one traveler"，以"我在那路口久久伫立"表达出诗人犹豫踟蹰的内心情感，在译文风格上与原作保持一致，文字处理细腻严谨。第二节的译文与原诗出入略大，译者直接省略了原诗中的"as just as fair"及"and having perhaps the better claim"，将第四句的"grassy"译为"荒草萋萋"，"wanted wear"译为"十分幽寂"，可见用词之斟酌。为达到结构工整，使译文与原文形式对等，增译一句"显得更诱人，更美丽"。这一处理提醒广大译者，译诗时不必句句对译，可合译相同或相似部分，也可省略赘余部分，切勿"困神于形"。后两句与原作出入较大，这两句的意思应当是在作者之后会有越来越多的人走上这条路，因而两条路也就逐渐没有什么差别。而译者在这两句的理解上略有偏差，有违忠实性。第三节中，译者考虑到下文的"in leaves"，将第一句的"lay"译成"落叶满地"，即"路上铺满落叶"的意思，十分精妙。"equally"原意为"平等地、公正地"，译者将其译为"都"，完美传达了原作含义。最后一节，原诗前两句的语序与中文语序及表达方式有所区别，译者调整语序，采用"归化法"使译文更加符合读者的思维。"telling"被译为"将往事回顾"，描绘了多年以后诗人回忆这件事时的画面。"and that has made all the difference"译为"从此决定了我一生的道路"，表达出每一个选择对人生产生的重要影响。

（2）

A Red Red Rose

Robert Burns

O my luve is like a red, red rose,
That's newly sprung in June;
O my luve is like the melodie
That's sweetly played in tune.

As fair thou art, my bonie lass,
So deep in luve am I;
And I will luve thee still, my dear,
Till a' the seas gang dry.

Till a' the seas gang dry, my dear,
And the rocks melt wi' the sun;
And I will luve thee still, my dear,
While the sands o'life shall run.

And fare thee weel, my only luve,
And fare thee weel a while;
And I will come again, my luve,
Tho' it were ten thousand mile!

【译文】

一朵红红的玫瑰

罗伯特·彭斯

呵,我的爱人像朵红红的玫瑰,
六月里迎风初开;
呵,我的爱人像支甜甜的曲子,
奏得合拍又和谐。

我的好姑娘,多么美丽的人儿!
请看我,多么深挚的爱情!
亲爱的,我永远爱你,
纵使大海干涸水流尽。

纵使大海干涸水流尽,
太阳将岩石烧为灰尘,
亲爱的,我永远爱你,
只要我一息犹存。

珍重吧,我唯一的爱人,
珍重吧,让我们暂时别离,
我定要回来,亲爱的,
哪怕跋千里万里。

【评析】 *A Red Red Rose* 是由苏格兰著名诗人罗伯特·彭斯于1794年创作的一首赞美爱人的情诗,发表于1796年。诗歌根据苏格兰古民歌改编而来,辞藻清新自然,宛如在爱人耳边低声吟唱的曲子。诗中运用了比喻、反复、排比等多种修辞手法,表达了主人公对爱人忠贞不渝的浓浓爱意。彭斯采用民谣体(ballad metre),使该诗既能吟诵,又可歌唱,这也是该诗流传至今,深受人们喜爱的原因。

标题有引领全诗,为诗歌奠定情感基调的作用。根据英译汉的一般规律,不定冠词(a、an)除了在表示"一"这个数量时需译出之外,其他情况通常不译。但在这首抒发对爱人情感的诗中，译者用"一朵"起到了缓慢节奏的作用，同时表达出作者的专一与诚意，使得整首诗的感情更加深沉浓厚。通常情况下，汉语多重复，而英语少用重复。在这里，英文标题重复了"red"，既强调了玫瑰鲜艳的色彩，又抒发对爱人缠绵的情感。译文同样使用重复的手法，译为"红红的玫瑰"，语气舒缓，音韵绵长，"红红"二字更显玫瑰惹人怜爱，起到强调作用。

第一节中，一、三两句使用对仗句式，"红红的玫瑰"和"甜甜的曲子"相呼应，颇具民歌反复吟唱的特点。乍看起来，原诗中这两句字数不同，译为对仗句有失形式美。但实际上，英诗不同于汉诗，不追求字数相等，只要音节相同即可，第一句和第三句都是十个音节，因此译为字数相同的对仗句并无大碍，反而增强了可读性和顺畅性。二、四两句都译为七个字，将"newly sprung"译作"迎风初开"，体现出一种动态的娇羞摇曳之感，花香袭人之媚态呼之欲出。但原诗这两句的韵脚并未在译诗中得到复现。第二节的第一句作为全诗的点睛之笔，贯穿全诗。诗人使用"我的好姑娘""多么美丽""人儿"一叠三叹，描绘出对心上人深切的感情。二、三句重复强调，最后一句与第三节首行相呼应，起承转合之间让读者感受到作者对心上人呼之欲出的浓浓情意。第四小节中，作者重复第三节中"亲爱的，我永远爱你"一行，表达了自己坚贞的爱情立场，"我定要回来"一句充满了海枯石烂的勇气，信念十分坚定。

Questions for Teacher's Lecture（讲解题）

Translate the following poems into Chinese.
（1）
Love's Secret
William Blake

Never seek to tell thy love,
Love that never told can be;

For the gentle wind does move
Silently, invisibly.

I told my love, I told my love,
I told her all my heart;
Trembling, cold, in ghastly fears,
Ah! she did depart!

Soon as she was gone from me,
A traveler came by,
Silently, invisibly
He took her with a sigh.

(2)

The Human Seasons

John Keats

Four Seasons fill the measure of the year;
    There are four seasons in the mind of Man:
He has his lusty Spring, when fancy clear
    Takes in all beauty with an easy span:
He has his Summer, when luxuriously
    Spring's honey'd cud of youthful thought he loves
To ruminate, and by such dreaming high
    Is nearest unto heaven: quiet coves
His soul has in its Autumn, when his wings
    He furleth close; contented so to look
On mists in idleness—to let fair things
    Pass by unheeded as a threshold brook—
He has his Winter too of pale misfeature,
    Or else he would forego his mortal nature.

(3)
Sheep in Fog
Sylvia Plath

The hills step off into whiteness.
People or stars
Regard me sadly, I disappoint them.

The train leaves a line of breath
O slow
Houses the colour of rust

Hooves, dolorous bells
All morning the
Morning has been blackening.

A flower left out,
My bones hold a stillness, the far
Fields melt my heart

They threaten
To let me through to a heaven
Starless and fatherless, a dark water.

Exercises for Students(练习题)

Translate the following poems into Chinese.
(1)
If I Can Stop One Heart from Breaking
Emily Dickinson
If I can stop one heart from breaking,

I shall not live in vain;

If I can ease one life the aching,

Or cool one pain,

Or help one fainting robin

Unto his nest again,

I shall not live in vain.

(2)

When You Are Old

William Butler Yeats

When you are old and grey and full of sleep,

And nodding by the fire, take down this book,

And slowly read, and dream of the soft look.

Your eyes had once, and of their shadows deep;

How many loved your moments of glad grace,

And loved your beauty with love false or true,

But one man loved the pilgrim Soul in you,

And loved the sorrows of your changing face;

And bending down beside the glowing bars,

Murmur, a little sadly, how Love fled.

And paced upon the mountains overhead,

And hid his face amid a crowd of stars.

(3)

Fire and Ice

Robert Frost

Some say the world will end in fire,

Some say in ice.

From what I've tasted of desire

I hold with those who favour fire.

But if it had to perish twice,
I think I know enough of hate
To say that for destruction ice
Is also great
And would suffice.

Versions for Appreciation（译文赏析）

（1）If people mean anything at all by the expression "untimely death", they must believe that some deaths run on a better schedule than others. Death in old age is rarely called untimely—a long life is thought to be a full one. But with the passing of a young person, one assumes that the best years lay ahead and the measure of that life was still to be taken.

History denies this, of course. Among prominent summer deaths, one recalls those of Marilyn Monroe and James Deans, whose lives seemed equally brief and complete. Writers cannot bear the fact that poet John Keats died at 26, and only half playfully judge their own lives as failures when they pass that year. The idea that the life cut short is unfilled is illogical because lives are measured by the impressions they leave on the world and by their intensity and virtue.

【译文】 如果人们借"英年早逝"这一字眼真的意欲表达什么含义的话，他们必然相信某些人的辞世可以算是寿终正寝，而另一些人则"死不逢时"。死于年迈很少被冠以"死不逢时"之名，因为能度过漫长的一生被认为是甚为圆满的。反之，如果所碰到的是一位年轻人之死，人们会以为这位年轻人风华正茂，前途无可限量，生命的倒计时尚未真正开始。

当然，历史否定这一切。在诸多较为著名的"英年早逝"的情形中，我们会忆起玛丽莲·梦露与詹姆斯·迪恩斯之死，其生命并不因其短暂而有损其圆满。对于约翰·济慈年方26便溘然长逝这一事实，文人墨客们皆痛不欲生，但他们中仅有半数人诙谐地认为，若他们也死于这一年龄，其一生可视为失败。视英年早逝为不圆满，这一观念有悖于逻辑，因为衡量生命的尺度乃是留给世界的印记，是生命的力度及其美德。

【评析】 本文是一篇典型的议论型语篇，用词正式，逻辑严谨，哲理性强。要很好地理解这类文章，需要有一定的推理能力。翻译时，要特别注意整篇文章的逻辑关系，注意上下文的衔接。第一句话句子结构其实很简单，但是由于内容比较抽象，理解和翻译起来还是有一定的难度。"untimely death"当然可以翻译为"过早的死亡"，但是如此表达过于直白，会破坏原文的语境，不如翻译成"英年早逝"，既把最基本的意思表达出来了，又给译文增色不少。"run on a better schedule"直译过来是"在一个更好的日程里奔跑"，但是这样翻译会让读者摸不着头脑，什么是更好的日程？为什么要奔跑？联系上下文可知，这里想表达的意思其实就是一些人的死亡比另外一些人要更合时宜。译文采用分译法，将这个句子分成两个短句，拓展开来详细说明。并且两个短句结尾都用到四字格，整齐对称，形成对比。第二段第一句中的"summer death"也值得好好品味，如果单看这一句话，理解起来可能不太容易。什么是"summer death"，是在夏天去世的人吗？当然不是，联系上下文可以推断出，这里的"summer death"其实就是指上文中出现的"untimely death"。英语中经常会变换着说法来表达同一件事物，在中文中则需要将它们统一起来，因此这里同样译为"英年早逝"。另外需要注意的是，翻译中词性的转换也非常重要，运用得好可以给译文锦上添花。原文中"playfully"是一个副词，但是译文却把它处理成一个形容词"痛不欲生"，词性的转换并没有对原文的情感造成任何损失，反而愈加饱满。最后一句被动语态的处理也是翻译中经常用到的方法。

（2）It is easy to underestimate English writer James Herriot. He had such a pleasant, readable style that one might think that anyone could imitate it. How many times have I heard people say, "I could write a book. I just haven't the time." Easily said. Not so easily done. James Herriot, contrary to popular opinion, did not find it easy in his early days of, as he put it, having a go at the writing game. While he obviously had an abundance of natural talent, the final, polished work that he gave to the world was the result of years of practising, re-writing and reading. Like the majority of authors, he had to suffer many disappointments and rejections along the way, but these made him all the more determined to succeed. Everything he achieved in life was earned the hard way and his success in the literary field was no exception.

【译文】 人们很容易低估英国作家吉米·哈利。他文笔风趣，文章可读性强，以至于有人觉得谁都能模仿。我曾无数次听人说："我也能写书，只是没有时间而已。"易说，做到却难。和大家的看法不同，吉米·哈利自己说，在初期"从事创作活动"并不容易。尽管他才华横溢，天赋异禀，但也经历了多年的写作实践、修订、审读，才最终为世人呈现出精雕细琢的作品。跟大多数作家一样，他这一路走来，也遭遇到无数次的失意和冷遇，但这些都使他更加坚定，走向成功。他一生中所取得的一切成就都来之不易，在文学领域的建树亦非例外。

【评析】 本文主要讲述了英国作家吉米·哈利克服困难，从事创作，最终取得成功的经历。文章开头较多引语，口语色彩重，比较简单，后半部分多为长句，翻译难度较大。第二句中的"style"原来是"风格"的意思，这里是指"写作风格，文风"，因此可以把"pleasant style"翻译为"文笔风趣"。而"readable"的意思是"可读的"，在中文里很少用来修饰文风，这里可以用增词法进行翻译，我们一般谈到文章时才会用到这个词，因此这里可以处理为"文章可读性强"。第三句中"how many times"后面用到了倒装语序，有明显的强调意味，可以翻译为"我曾无数次听人说"。第六句中"have a go"是一个固定搭配，这个词组的翻译有一定的难度，它的意思是"尝试做某事，开始着手做某事"。而"writing game"不宜直译为"写作游戏"，这样会破坏整个中文的语境，翻译成"创作活动"最为通顺，这样，上文的"having a go"不仅可以译为"尝试"，还可以译为"从事"。由此看来，不管是句子翻译还是语篇翻译，都要做到瞻前顾后，统筹全局。第七句的翻译为全篇最佳，接连用到了三个四字格成语，原文意思传递到位，首尾呼应，读起来朗朗上口。短短一句话，三个成语信手拈来，没有深厚的文学功底，一般人很难做到。最后一句话同样体现了善用四字格的妙处，如果将前半句译为"他一生所取得的一切成就是不容易得到的"就会显得有点啰嗦，不如直接把"was earned the hard way"译为"来之不易"，句子更加精简且句意同样完整。

（3）A fifth grader gets a homework assignment to select his future career path from a list of occupations. He ticks "astronaut" but quickly adds "scientist" to the list and selects it as well. The boy is convinced that if he reads enough, he can explore as many career paths as he likes. And so he reads—everything from encyclopedias to science fiction novels. He reads so passionately that his parents have to institute a "no reading policy" at the dinner table.

That boy was Bill Gates, and he hasn't stopped reading yet—not even after becoming one of the most successful people on the planet. Nowadays, his reading material has changed from science fiction and reference books: recently, he revealed that he reads at least 50 nonfiction books a year. Gates chooses nonfiction titles because they explain how the word works.

"Each book opens up new avenues of knowledge," Gates say.

【译文】 有一名五年级的学生收到了一份家庭作业，要他在一系列职业清单中选出自己未来的职业之路。他选了"宇航员"，但是随即又迅速在单子上加了个"科学家"，并且也选上了。这个男孩相信，如果书读得够多，他就能随心所欲地探索尽可能多的职业道路。因此，他博览群书——无论是百科全书还是科幻小说。他如此痴迷于阅读，以至于父母不得不规定他吃饭时"禁止阅读"。

这个男孩就是比尔·盖茨，他还没有停止阅读——哪怕自己已然成为这个世界最成功的人之一。如今，他阅读的材料不再是科幻类小说和工具类书籍。最近，他透露自己一年至少要读50本非小说类书籍。盖茨选择非小说类书籍，是因为它们可以解释世界是如何运转的。

"每一本书都会打开探索知识的新道路。"盖茨说道。

第 8 章　Translation of Discourse（语篇翻译）

【评析】　这篇文章主要讨论的是比尔·盖茨一直爱好读书，即使功成名就，依然保持着阅读习惯。文章故事性强，总体难度不大。文章第一句以不定冠词开头，有讲故事的意味，翻译时最好加上一个"有"字，符合中文的写作习惯。"convince"本来有"使相信；说服"的意思，但是第三句中"be convinced that"是习惯用法，意思为"相信，确信"，不能翻译为"被说服"。第四句有点特殊，整个句子的主语和谓语是"he reads"，破折号后的"everything"是"reads"的宾语，为了强调"everything"，同时也对"he reads"进行解释说明，所以用破折号隔开了。为了避免啰嗦，翻译时将"everything"和"he reads"放在一起，处理为"博览群书"，同样强调了读书之多，也凸显了译者的文化素养。第八句中的"title"一词需要注意，它的原意是"题目，标题"，这里指的是"书"。因此，"nonfiction titles"指的就是上文中提到的"nonfiction books"。英语中用不同单词表达同一种事物的现象很常见，这是一种语篇衔接的方式，目的是避免重复，在译成中文时则需要统一指代，这也是很多译者很少会注意的一点。最后一句话翻译出来容易，翻译好却并不简单。这句话用了引号，说明是盖茨说的话。既然是名人名言，翻译的时候可以适当进行文学处理。译文用到了增词法，添加了一个动词"探索"，读起来通顺且不失文学意味。

（4）It is simple enough to say that since books have classes—fiction, biography, poetry—we should separate them and take from each what it is right that each should give us. Yet few people ask for books what books can give us. Most commonly we come to books with blurred and divided minds，asking of fiction that it shall be true, of poetry that it shall be false，of biography that it shall be flattering, of history that it shall enforce our own prejudices. If we could banish all such preconceptions when we read, that would be an admirable beginning. Do not dictate to your author; try to become him. Being his fellow-worker and accomplice. If you hang back, and reserve and criticize at first, you are preventing yourself from getting the fullest possible value from what you read. But if you open your mind as widely as possible, then signs and hints of almost imperceptible fineness, from the twist and turn of the first sentences, will bring you into the presence of a human being unlike any other. Steep yourself in this, acquaint yourself with this, and soon you will find that your author is giving you, or attempting to give you, something far more definite.

【译文】 既然书有小说、传记、诗歌之分，我们就应把它们分类，从各类书中汲取其应该给予我们的营养。这话说来很简单。然而很少有人要求从书籍中得到它们所能提供的养分。我们总是三心二意地带着模糊的观念去看书，要求小说必须真实，要求诗歌必须虚构，要求传记阿谀逢迎，要求史书能加强自己的偏见。读书时如能抛开这些先入之见，便是极好的开端。不要对作者指手画脚，而要尽力与作者融为一体，共同构思，共同创作。如果你不参与，不投入，而且一开始就百般挑剔，那你就无缘从书中获得最大益处。你若敞开心扉，虚怀若谷，那么书中精细入微的寓意和暗示便会把你从开头那些山回水转般的句子中带出来，走到一个独特的人物面前。钻进去熟悉它，你很快就会发现，作者展示给你的或想要展示给你的是一些比原先要明确得多的东西。

【评析】 本文选自英国作家弗吉尼亚·伍尔夫的《怎样读书》一文。文章阐述了对如何读书的看法，虽用词简单，但内容深刻，读后令人感到意味深长。翻译时，需要从深层次上理解原文，然后在此基础上遣词造句。本文第一句话句子成分较多，翻译前首先要统观全句，正确分析成分之间的关系。这句话是一个强调句，"It"是形式主语，真正的主语是"to say that..."，该句强调的部分是"that"引导的宾语从句。翻译时可以采用分译法，将宾语从句和主句的内容分别译成两个独立句，置于句首和句末。此外，将"it is simple to say"放在句末，同时与下一句的转折"yet"连贯起来，起到了承上启下的作用。翻译第三句时，需要注意"come to"这个表达，若将其简单理解为"来到，参加"或者"恢复，苏醒"则语义会不通顺。翻译时需要根据上下文来理解，这句话说的是阅读书籍过程中的一种心态，因此"come to book"可以理解为"阅读图书"或"捧起书籍"。将"blurred and divided minds"译为"三心二意"可谓是点睛之笔，不仅将意思精准地传递了出来，而且用到了四字格成语，言简意赅，发人深省。最后，在翻译"signs and hints of almost imperceptible fineness"时需要注意，"almost imperceptible fineness"是"signs and hints"的后置定语，应当按照中文表达习惯将定语置于其所修饰的名词前，翻译成"精细入微的寓意和暗示"。

8.2　Translation of Scientific Writings（科技语篇的翻译）

科技语篇是指以介绍自然科学科学研究成果为主的文章或著作。这种文体往往专业术语多，专业性强，分析客观、具体，结构严密完整，逻辑性强，句式严整，少有变化，其文体与修辞手段在许多方面有别于文学等文体。

1. 词汇特点

1）大量的科技词汇或专门术语

科技语篇中存在大量的科技术语和专门词汇，如：化学领域中的 isotope（同位素），物理领域的 photon（光子），以及生物领域的 chromosome（染色体）等。

2）借用大量的外来词

部分科技英语词汇来源于外来语，其中拉丁语、希腊语对英语科技词汇的影响源远流长。

3）新造词汇不断出现

科技发展带来了新事物的出现，新概念的生成，新事物、新概念又带来词汇的创造和增加。随着网络的出现，有了 cyber、email 等，后来有了克隆技术，又有了 clone。

4）根据构词法而来的派生词、合成词比例非常大

科技语篇中有大量的派生词和合成词，例如由前缀法构成的 antimissile（反导弹），microchemistry（微量化学）等，和由后缀法构成的以 -logy 结尾的词表示某学科的词 futurology（未来学），planetology（太阳系星体学）等。

5）广泛运用缩略词语

缩略语简单易记，在科技英语中使用普遍，如 DNA（脱氧核糖核酸），IC（集成电路），UPS（不间断电源），MOS（金属氧化物半导体）等。

2. 句法特点

1）大量使用被动结构

被动结构的广泛使用是科技英语最为显著的特征，这样避免了不必要的人称代词，使句子结构更加紧凑。如：

（1）When this air has been exhausted, an area of low pressure is created near it.

【译文】 这些空气被耗尽后附近形成一个低压区。

【评析】 如果把动词"exhausted"和"created"的主语补充出来，句子会显得累赘，所以译文直接使用被动语态。

（2）All these factors can be expressed as complex mathematical equations which can be solved by a computer to give the optimum equipment minimum cost.

【译文】 所有这些因素可以表示为复杂的数学方程式，这些方程式可用计算机算出，并求出最佳设备的最低成本。

【评析】 直接以"factor"作为主语，更能突出所要论证及说明的关键词，使读者立即可以明白句子所讨论的对象是这些"因素"的表示方法。

2）名词化倾向

大量使用名词化结构（Nominalization）是科技英语的特点之一。例如：普通英语中会表达为 If machines are tested by this method, there will be some loss of power. 。科技英语则会表达为 The testing of machine by this method entails some loss of power. 。这种表达用词简洁，结构紧凑，在很多情况下可省略过多的主谓结构，故在科技英语作品中非常常用。

（1）Television is the transmission and reception of images of moving objects by radio waves.

【译文】 电视通过无线电波发射和接收活动物体的图像。

(2) Since 95 percent of the finding on unidentified flying objects have been explained as signs of nature, these signs should be explained to people.

【译文】 既然发现的不明飞行物中,有95%被解释为自然征兆,那么就应该向人们解释这些征兆。

3)陈述句多,时态种类有限

科技英语中,作者只是客观陈述事实和问题,描写过程和状态,说明功能和特征,所论事理多具有一般性、频繁性和特征性。行文时以直接叙述为主,多采用一般现在时或一般过去时,间或也使用现在完成时以表示与现在有直接联系。

4)长句多

科技英语中长而复杂的难句有很多。在标准资料、专利说明书和规范等文献类型中尤为多见。长句中常是一个主句带若干从句和非谓语动词短语,从句带短语,短语带从句,从句套从句,互相依附,相互制约。

5)依式行文,文笔朴素,修辞手法单调

科技英语中使用的修辞手法比较单调。在行文格式上,科技语篇总是开门见山,直截了当,把要表达的主要信息尽量前置,使读者能立即抓住问题的重点。翻译时,译者应多查字典,翻阅有关资料和书籍,或者请教熟悉专业的人员。

考虑到科技语篇的修辞特点,在翻译时要注意不可过分拘泥于原文形式。翻译科技作品,主要任务是正确清楚表达原文的内容。衡量科技文献翻译质量的标准应是看译文是否具有正确性、一致性、连贯性和完整性。要多查专业书籍、资料,问专业人员,彻底弄懂,然后再动笔翻译,这样才能保证译文质量。

Versions for Appreciation(译文赏析)

(1) And in the vicinity of the sun a good deal of the blue light is reflected back into space by the finer dust, thus giving a yellowish tinge to that which reaches us reflected chiefly from the coarse dust of the lower

atmosphere. At sunset and sunrise, however, this last effect is greatly intensified, owing to the great thickness of the strata of air through which the light reaches us. The enormous amount of this dust is well shown by the fact that only then can we look full at the sun, even when the whole sky is free from clouds and there is no apparent mist.

【译文】 在太阳附近，大量的蓝光被细微的尘埃反射回天空，所以，由低空大气层粗粒尘埃反射到地面的光线便带有浅黄色。在日出日落时，由于光线到达地面需要穿过厚厚的大气层，这种反射效果大大增强了。只有在这种时候我们才可以直视太阳，即使是万里长空，没有一点云彩，没有一丝雾霭。这就充分显示了低空中尘埃数量之大。

【评析】 此段摘自一篇科普文，在翻译此类长难句时，首先要注意划分句子结构，对句意有整体的把握，力求忠实通顺。第一句中"thus giving a yellowish tinge to that which"直译为"因而使照射到地面的光线呈浅黄色"，其中"that"为指示代词，指代"the light"，后面的"reflected"部分是过去分词短语做后置定语修饰"that"。第二句在翻译时将句尾的原因状语移至主句前面，使之更加符合汉语表达习惯。第三句汉译时采用了拆分译法，将同位语从句"that only then can we look full at the sun"译成独立句，并调整语序，将同位语从句和让步状语从句移至主句前，其中的短语"look full at the sun"译为"直视太阳"。

（2）So it is necessary to understand the main issues involved in ESD protection circuit design and the physical mechanisms taking place in order to ensure that the design can be scaled or transferred with minimum impact to the ESD performance.

【译文】 因此，为了能够改变设计的大小比例或者转移设计，并且对ESD性能的影响最小，我们必须理解ESD保护电路设计中的主要问题和电路物理原理。

【评析】 英语的叙事顺序有时与汉语的顺序恰恰相反，汉语通常是前因后果，而英语则是前果后因。因此在翻译时译者须对此类句型进行语序调整，将目的状语从句"in order to..."从主句中拆分出来放到句首来译，以表原因。同时，在处理目的状语从句中的附加成分"with..."时也采用了拆分法，将其译成一个独立的分句，突出了其强调的作用。

（3）In fact, any measurement below room temperature comes into the area of low temperature physics, but it has become a common practice to take low temperature physics as the physics research carried out at temperatures below about 90 K（degree Kelvin）, which can be taken from the scale whose absolute zero of temperature is at 0 K, corresponding to -459.6 ℉, or -237.2 ℃.

【译文】 实际上，任何低于室温的度量都属于低温物理学的范畴。但是，通常习惯于把低温物理学看成是在温度等于或低于氧的沸点，亦即在温度低于 90 K（开氏绝对温度）时所进行的物理研究。这类温度可用开氏绝对温标测取，该温标的绝对零度为 0 K，相当于 -459.6 ℉ 或 -237.2 ℃。

【评析】 在处理该语段时，应注意以下几个问题：首先，逻辑关系要译清楚，从整个句子来看，前后两个分句之间有一层"严格"与"普通"的对比关系，因此，需要把表达这种关系的词语提到句首，使之形成对比。同时，连接词"but"的转折关系要表达清楚。其次，词义选择要准确无误。"common practice" 在这里不是常识，而是指"习惯做法"。"scale" 结合上下文来看，具体指的是"Kelvin absolute scale"。最后，表达时考虑到中文阅读习惯，不宜将句子译得过长，可考虑将两个定语从句译为分句。

（4）The nutritional requirements of fish are similar to those of land animals for growth, reproduction, and other normal physiological functions they need to consume protein, minerals, vitamins and growth factors, and every source.

【译文】 为了生长、繁殖及维持其他正常生理机能，鱼和陆地上的动物一样，需要蛋白质、矿物质、维生素和生长素，以及各种能量。

【评析】 英语词汇通常具有一词多义的现象，这就为词义的正确选择增加了难度。因此在翻译时，不能单从词的表面意义入手，需要译者从逻辑分析入手，识别原文中词汇的感情色彩和文体风格，如词义褒贬、词的通俗或正式、口语或书面等。科技文体中，需选择词义严谨，符合专业特征，能与上下文匹配的词，如句中的"reproduction"不可译为"再生产"，根据句意，应译为"生殖、繁殖"才符合原文意思。

（5）It (wood frog) spends its winters interned in subzero sleep, its tissues steel-rigid, and revives in the spring raring to go. It's the Rip Van Winkle of the animal world.

【译文】 在冬天，它（林蛙）的体温降到零度以下，处于休眠状态，器官组织没有任何活动，而到了春天，它就会复活。它是动物界的瑞普·凡·温克尔。

【评析】 此段选自科普类著作，近年来，此类作品通常结合文学与科技文体的特点，目的是以简单、通俗、易懂的词汇和语句向大众普及科学知识，通常会采用一些修辞手法，如明喻、隐喻、拟人等，使文章更加生动具体，因此常常具有通俗性和趣味性。此句中，作者使用隐喻的修辞手法，将林蛙比作瑞普·凡·温克尔。 温克尔是美国作家华盛顿·欧文著名短篇小说中的主人公，因喝了仙酒后入睡，醒来下山后才发现时间已经过了整整二十年，沧海桑田，世界早已不是从前的样子。译者在翻译时，也需采用同样的修辞手法，形象生动地将原本枯燥难懂的科技文再现出来。但不可多做虚饰，应力求忠于原文，通顺易懂。同时，也要注重百科知识积累，以防遇到陌生内容，从而影响译文质量。

（6）But Japan spent roughly $3 billion, and is considered the international leader in most optic field.

【译文】 但日本却花费了约 30 亿美元，而且人们认为它在光学的大多数领域居国际领先地位。

【评析】 科技文体一般语言规范，逻辑清晰，客观准确。被动句的特定句式结构符合科技文体的特征，因此，为达到严谨可靠的目的，科技文中常采用被动语态。如果英语中以宾语或宾语补语的动词做被动语态的谓语时，往往会省略施事者，在翻译过程中，译者可添加

"人们、我们、众人"等泛指性词汇做主语。此句中"is considered"为被动语态,"Japan"是真正的宾语,翻译时增加"人们"将其译为主动句。因前一句出现过"日本",在第二句中可用"它"指代,使译文更加简洁明了。

Questions for Teacher's Lecture(讲解题）

Translate the following passages into Chinese.

(1) Modern scientific research show that tea helps dissipate internal heat and ameliorate digestion, micturition and secretion of saliva. If refreshes one, helps him regain physical energy and relieve him of fatigue. Facts demonstrate the prompt exhilarating effect of a cup of hot tea after physical or mental labor. A cup of hot tea can even cool himself down on a hot summer day. With its caffeine content, tea also stimulates the nerves and muscles and promotes metabolism. Besides, strong tea works well after a rich meal due to the fast dissolving effect of its aromatic oil composition.

(2) A magnetic compass is an instrument showing direction based on the phenomenon that a magnetic bar or needle swinging freely in the earth's magnetic field will direct itself to lie in a magnetic south-north position. It differs from the south-pointing chariot in that the latter has differential gearing. The term "compass" in this article includes all the various models in different historical periods, among them there are the Sinan, the Zhinanyu (South-pointing fish) and the Zhinanzhen (South-pointing needle). The inventor and the exact invention dates remain unknown, but it is clear that the primitive magnetic south-pointing instrument appeared very early in China as a result of the knowledge people gained over long years of labor.

Exercises for Students（练习题）

Translate the following passages into Chinese.

（1）

Some medical historians have implicated kidney disease because of Mozart's malformed ear. Ears and kidneys develop at about the same time in the human embryo; hence, a malformed ear may indicate problems with the kidneys as well. But Mozart had no history of renal dysfunction, Fitzgerald says. And advanced kidney disease produces delirium earlier in the course of illness.

So Fitzgerald settles at last on congestive heart failure, which can cause anasarca if the heart can't pump enough blood through the kidneys to eliminate fluid retaining salts. Heart troubles would be easy to confirm with any one of the stethoscopes that adorn audience members at Davidge Hall. "Unfortunately," says Fitzgerald, "Mozart died more than a quarter of a century before the invention of stethoscope. And there was no description of his doctor's leaning an ear against his heart to listen to it. If I were facing a really swollen, febrile, rash, sweaty guy, I might not want to put my ear on his chest either."

Fitzgerald notes, however, that at the time of Mozart's death an epidemic of rheumatic fever is said to have besieged Vienna. Rheumatic fever is triggered by an invading bacterium that elicits antibodies from the immune system. The antibodies attack the bacterium, but they can also attack tissue in a vulnerable host's own heart, skin, joints, and brain. This reaction can cause congestive heart failure, Fitzgerald points out, as well as the rest of Mozart's physical symptoms. And chorea, the neurological consequence of rheumatic fever, could account for Mozart's final delirium, as well as the puzzling change of character that prompted him to drive his pet canary out of the sickroom days before his passing.

(2)

But why did so many people love the music, yet recoil when they discovered how it was composed? A study by computer scientist David Moffat of Glasgow Caledonian University provides a clue. He asked both expert musicians and non-experts to assess six compositions. The participants weren't told beforehand whether the tunes were composed by humans or computers, but were asked to guess, and then rate how much they liked each one. People who thought the composer was a computer tended to dislike the piece more than those who believed it was human. This was true even among the experts, who might have been expected to be more objective in their analyses.

Where does this prejudice come from? Paul Bloom of Yale University has a suggestion: he reckons part of the pleasure we get from art stems from the creative process behind the work. This can give it an "irresistible essence", says Bloom. Meanwhile, experiments by Justin Kruger of New York University have shown that people's enjoyment of an artwork increases if they think more time and effort was needed to create it. Similarly, Colton thinks that when people experience art, they wonder what the artist might have been thinking or what the artist is trying to tell them. It seems obvious, therefore, that with computers producing art, this speculation is cut short—there's nothing to explore. But as technology becomes increasingly complex, finding those greater depths in computer art could become possible. This is precisely why Colton asks the Painting Fool to tap into online social networks for its inspiration: hopefully this way it will choose themes that will already be meaningful to us.

8.3　Translation on Practical Writings（应用文语篇的翻译）

应用文也称实用文体，是直接传递信息或提供服务的语篇，其对象明确、范畴广泛、格式固定、语言得体，文字简洁且时效性强，讲究实效。从信函通告到条约公文都属于应用文的范畴，常见的应用文体包括公私信函、通知公告、规章法令、广告海报、法律文书、契约合同、启示通报等。尽管其种类繁多，但行文多以书面语为主，措辞严谨，句式整齐，往往具有特定的文本样式和表达模式。

译者要力求客观，避免个人感情的渗入，以传递信息为主。翻译时注意要用词恰当、言简意赅、条理清晰、表达准确、通俗易懂。以下是《关于个人数据自动化处理的个人保护公约》中英文版本的节选，属于条约型应用文。

（1）Each Party shall provide that the controller, and, where applicable the processor, takes appropriate security measures against risks such as accidental or unauthorized access to, destruction, loss, use, modification or disclosure of personal data.

【译文】 各缔约方应当规定控制者以及处理者（若适用）采取适当的安全措施防范，如个人数据的意外或未经授权的访问、损坏、丢失、使用、修改或披露。

（2）Each Party shall provide that the controller notifies, without delay, at least the competent supervisory authority within the meaning of Article 15 of this Convention, of those data breaches which may seriously interfere with the rights and fundamental freedoms of data subjects.

【译文】 各缔约方应当规定数据控制者至少立即向本公约第十五条所指范围内的主管监管机构通报可能严重妨碍数据主体的权利和基本自由的数据泄露。

通过这个例子，不难发现应用文体的语言特点及翻译时需要注意的问题。

1）开门见山、自然质朴

应用文语言直接质朴，少用修饰，侧重于"以事告人"。语言上重视语法、逻辑和专业术语的准确性。上述例文使用的是正式书面体，语言正式、严谨。

2）文有定型、约定俗成

应用文行文需符合固定格式，多用惯用语。标题、开头、结尾、转折及过渡一般有固定程式和用语。译者在翻译时，需要注意形式问题，在格式、体例方面需与原文保持一致。

3）确切无误、明白通晓

应用文通常具有很强的时效性和实用性。要求语言简单明确，通俗易懂，可短时间内执行、答复或办理文中内容，切忌模棱两可，歪曲事实。在翻译时应力求准确，不得掺杂个人情感，避免不规范的用语。

4）言简意赅、文约事丰

基于时效性的前提，应用文通常以简约凝练的文字高效传达信息，以节省时间、提高办事效率。译文不求华美优雅，而是言简意赅地传达原文内容，准确明晰。

5）文字数据、表格图形

一般文章多用文字表述，应用文除了使用文字表述外，还可以用数据、表格、图形来说明事实，特别是财经类应用文。在数字翻译时，对于纯粹属于计量或统计范畴的数值，译文一般使用阿拉伯数字，如 fifty million 可译为 5000 万。原文用英文数字或罗马数字表示的，除纯粹属于计量或统计范畴数值的情况外，译文用汉字，如 twenty-fourth committee 可译为二十四国委员会。

6）有声有色、活泼鲜明

明白显露、直来直去、言简意明、语言庄重是应用文的基本要求。但在调查报告、广告语、邀请信中也可以用生动活泼的语言表达事理、吸引读者。

简言之，应用文翻译需全面把握原文语言和文体风格，准确无误地传达原文信息，应与文学翻译相区分。以下对信函、广告、合同等三种类型加以详解。

1. 信函翻译

信函在人类的交流与沟通中起着重要作用。英文信函通常具有特定的格式和行文要求，其语言特点可简单归纳为4个C。

1）清楚（Clarity）

清楚是指一封信的内容一般着重说明一两件事，段落分明，层次清楚，主题突出，使对方一目了然。要注意表达清晰，用词要简易，忌用大词或生僻词。一旦用词不当，会造成表达上的晦涩与不清晰，令人难以理解。

2）简洁（Conciseness）

简洁是指必要的事项皆需一一说清，无关之事只字不提，避免内容冗长。翻译时，应在清楚和礼貌的基础上用最简洁的语言传递信息。特别是一些高效的商业信函更应该表达准确，要点清晰。

3）准确（Correctness）

准确指用词准确达意，语法行文正确规范，避免使用过多的修饰词。在商务信函中，应特别注意对于数量、日期和方式等信息的翻译，以免出现失误。同时，由于英汉两种语言在信函结构程式上有一定的区别，如收寄人的地址、写信时间及其呈现位置是不一样的，在翻译时要做出适当调整，以适应目的语的格式规范。例如：把英文地址由小到大的顺序译为汉语的由大到小的顺序。

4）礼貌（Courtesy）

礼貌指书信语言应用词得体文雅，语气礼貌，不得给人虚伪之感，结尾需有结束语和签名。

Versions for Appreciation（译文赏析）

Mr. An Kang

requests the pleasure of the company of

Mr. Mrs. T. S. Black

at dinner

at 7.00 p.m. on Monday, 12th June

at 10 Westcombe Park Road, London SE3 R.S.V.P.

Tel. 03-454-5802

Dress: Formal

【译文】

请柬

谨定于 6 月 12 日（星期一）下午 7 时在伦敦东南三邮区威斯特寇姆公园路 10 号举行晚宴，敬请布莱克先生和夫人届时光临！

敬请回复。

安康

电话：03-454-5802

服装：礼服

【评析】 请柬（帖）（包括接受邀请、谢却邀请）属于社交信函，翻译时主要是时间、地点、事项及格式问题。翻译时应按照汉语请柬的格式规范，对语言及格式稍做调整，不必局限于原文格式，可适当增加如"谨定于"或"届时光临"等汉语词汇。

不同于私人信函，公函主要指正式的或官方的书信，是用于日常信息、事务交流商洽的书面文体，使用范围较广，行文正式严谨。这种文体大都有固定的格式，按固定程式行文，有函头（heading）、受函人地址（inside address）、称呼（salutation）、函件正文（body）、结束语（closing sentence）函尾套语（complementary closing）、致函人签名（signature）。另外，有些公函在称呼下还要写上标题（caption）或参照（reference），其主要部分是函件正文。

公函多用于公事磋商、公务答询、团体联系等，往往涉及愿望、允诺、赞许、建议、催促、询问、拒绝、辩解或申述、质问、谴责。公函文体中情态动词比较多，在表达上一般都比较婉转含蓄，尽力保持公事公办的持重感（businesslike poise），常用文言词语或正式书面语，如"收悉、承蒙、见告、特此函询、请即复函"等。函件中情态虽常有变化，但一般较为婉转，翻译时要考虑语气特点。公函译文总的要求是简明、严谨、准确，特别是事实细节，如日期、数量、代号等，不可有所疏漏。

Versions for Appreciation（译文赏析）

Dear Sirs,

June 8, 2017

You have no doubt received Mr. Charles H. Black's letter of May 19, in which he advised you that the writer who has charge of our export business would write to you regarding builder's hardware and other items that are reported in great demand at present in China. Due to the abundance of stock of all types of merchandise such as builder's hardware, carpenter's tools, etc. in their superior qualities, we are in a position to do export business advantageously to you. We are now working on a new catalog, which you will shortly receive by separate mail.

We are keeping your letter on file and write you later how we could arrange to handle this business on a credit basis that would be satisfactory to all concerned.

Sincerely yours,

American Hardware Company

John Combray

Export Department

【译文】

尊敬的阁下：

5月19日布莱克先生之函已收悉。信函告知贵方当前中国市场急需大量建筑用五金产品，我公司为该项出口业务的承办人。由于我公司现有各种建筑五金及其他产品，如木工工具等存货，品质上乘。我方愿意在互利的基础上与贵方达成交易。目前我方正编印新的产品目录，将另函附邮，不日可达。

我方已将贵方的函件存档，并将进一步联系，以期在双方诚信互利的基础上达成协议。

美国五金公司国际贸易部

约翰·康布雷　敬呈

2017 年 6 月 8 日

【评析】　这是一份关于建立商务来往关系的商务公函,由称谓语、日期、正文、结束语及签名等五部分组成。鉴于商业交流的习惯和要求,行文应简洁明了、主题明确、就事论事,译文恰好体现了其内容的简明性。在翻译时,原文信息必须完整具体,涉及双方的利益和责任的内容要准确无误,还需注意句子的语法结构、逻辑关系、遣词(特别是数字)及标点符号的准确性。同时,要注意运用商业惯用语。通常来讲,商业信函里有很多常用的套语,在翻译时正确套用即可。英语商业信函里使用最常用的称呼是"Dear/sir/sirs",仅用于男性,"Dear Madam or Ladies",仅用于女性。汉语惯用的称呼语是"尊敬的阁下/先生"或"女士/夫人"。同样,结尾套语在英语里常用"Yours truly""Faithfully yours"或"Sincerely yours"等,汉语里则可译为"××谨呈/谨上"等。

2. 广告翻译

广告,顾名思义,就是广而告之,向公众告知或介绍某个产品、某件事物,是一种常用的应用文。商业广告最为常见,其通过媒体向消费者推销产品、吸引顾客、扩大市场需求。根据这一特点,广告内容通常采用褒扬溢美之词,使用较多的形容词及副词来描述产品形状、大小、品质等特征。用语通俗易懂、简短利落,少用结构复杂的长难句,有时甚至只有短短几个字便可达到宣传的效果。语言具有感召力、比较大众化、口语化,修辞上多用头韵、并列、夸张、重复、对仗等手段,形式别致新颖,引人注目,时态多采用一般现在时,清楚明了,通俗易懂。

在翻译广告时,既要保证语言信息的传递,又要考虑到广告所面对的文化环境。为了达到最佳效果,翻译时常常要打破原广告的语言形式,用目标人群易接受、好理解、喜闻乐见的语言形式和习惯表达出来。因此,在形式上要善于运用合适的修辞手法来体现并保留中英文各自的风格与语言特色。译文力求准确明了,优美生动,朗朗上口。在内容上,要了解文化差异和审美差别,及时调整译文,使译文与原文保持同样的广告效果。可多使用醒目易懂的简单句，语言凝练的省略句，朗朗上口的并列句以及感情强烈的祈使句等来达到说服他人购买，扩大知名度的目的。

Versions for Appreciation（译文赏析）

（1）Not all cars are created equal.

【译文】 并非所有的汽车都有相同的品质。

【评析】 这是三菱汽车开拓美国市场时的英语广告词。它套用了美国《独立宣言》中的首句"All men are created equal."。广告商将原句中的"men"改为"cars"来说明主体，并将原来的肯定句式改为否定句式，突出汽车的质量优势。由于这句话本身就家喻户晓，容易让人记住，因此产品在美国成功打开销路。广告商十分重视文化背景，使用习语，一语双关地打破了文化、地域、价值观等多重障碍，成功抓住消费者的心理，使之在思想上产生共鸣。在中国，三菱汽车这则广告被巧妙地译成"并非所有的汽车都有相同的品质"，而不是直译成"并非所有的汽车在被创造时就平等"。汽车作为产品，消费者更看重的是质量，且中国的消费者可能并不熟悉美国《独立宣言》中的话，所以如果直译，不但突显不出原文的含义，反而变得更加晦涩难懂，产生歧义。

（2）Every kid should have an Apple after school.

【译文】 每个孩子放学回家都该有个"苹果"。

【评析】 这是美国苹果电脑的广告。"apple"一词采用双关的手法，指孩子们放学后需要吃一个苹果来增强免疫力，补充能量，同样也暗示孩子们需要一台苹果电脑来放松身心，益智休闲。使用双关手法既引人注意又引人联想，生动幽默地加深了产品在潜在消费者心中的印象。

（3）Where there is a way, there is a Toyota.

【译文】 车到山前必有路，有路必有丰田车。

【评析】 这是日本丰田车的广告语，熟悉英语习语的人都知道这则广告汲取了英文中的"Where there is a will, there is a way."的结构。由于人们对于名言通常较为熟悉，因此这句广告非常利于大众记忆，但消费者需要购车时，脑海中会不自觉浮现这句广告词。而其到了中国则翻译成"车到山前必有路，有路必有丰田车"，这则中文广告词同样套用了中国的一句俗语，给中国消费者留下了深刻印象。该广告在目的论的基础上，以读者为中心，重视中国的文化背景，用传统习语对广告进行释义，给受众留下深刻的印象并产生积极的影响，从而实现广告的商业目的。

（4）Your lips will know it. But your hips won't show it.

【译文】 好吃看不见。

【评析】 这是一个巧克力品牌的广告词。直译为"你的嘴巴了解它，你的屁股不显现。"乍看来，这样既保留了原文的内容，又保留了原文的形式。但却给人一种不明所以的感觉，并未准确传达原文内涵，且用词不文雅，不适合在公众间流传。而"好吃看不见"突破了原广告的形式，仅用短短5个字就可突出该巧克力好吃且又不会令人发胖的特点。言简意赅，朗朗上口，容易被消费者记忆和接受，起到了广告的宣传效果。

3. 合同翻译

合同属于法律性文件，是当事双方设立、变更、终止某种关系的协议，具有合法性、平等性、目的性及普遍性。合同大都有较严格的格式要求，从语言结构上看，长句多，各类短语和从句都具有很强的限定作用。合同一般不讲究文采和修辞。这就要求译者在翻译时将准确严谨作为首要目标，尤其是涉及法律义务和专业术语时更应予以重视。译者必须要对原文内容实质有透彻的理解，绝不可歪曲事实，也不可随意增减内容。尽量不要对原句结构进行较大的改动、调整或断句，以免因结构变化而产生意义上的差异甚至漏洞。

同时，翻译时，要简单、扼要地阐明合同具体内容。同时也要避免使用方言和俚语，多使用官方认可的规范化语言或书面语。

Versions for Appreciation（译文赏析）

This contract is made by and between the authorized representatives of HASTINGS Ltd.（hereinafter called the Buyer）and the TAIHUA Industries Corporation（hereinafter called the Seller）through friendly discussion according to the terms and conditions stipulated thereunder.

【译文】 赫斯汀有限公司（以下简称买方）授权的代表与泰华工业公司（以下简称卖方）通过友好协商根据以下条款签订本合同。

【评析】 原文是完整的一个长句，句中无标点将句子断开。译文基本上是按照原文的句子结构而译，同为一句。按照汉语的表达习惯，将原文中的"This contract is made"从句首调整到句末，译为"签订本合同"。

Questions for Teacher's Lecture（讲解题）

Translate the following passages into Chinese.

（1）

Letter of Certificate

To Whom It May Concern,

This is to certify that Ms. Chris Tian has been employed in our office for the past five years. She is well acquainted with book-keeping. She has faithfully attended to her duties and proved herself thoroughly reliable. Any inquiries regarding her will be answered by.

Yours sincerely,

Kobe Hall

Chief Manager

（2）

Thank you for your letter of September suggesting that we grant you sole agency for our household linens. I regret to say that, at this stage, such an arrangement would be rather premature. We would, however, be willing to engage in a trial collaboration with you company to see how the arrangement works. It would be necessary for you to test the market for our products at your end. You would also have to build up a much larger turnover to justify a sole agency. We enclose price lists covering all the products you are interested in and look forward to hearing from you soon.

(3)

It is customary to insure goods against the risks of the journey. These risks include collision, leakage, pilferage, fire and storm, etc. If goods are properly insured, neither the exporter nor the customer suffers any loss. The passing of risk should be arranged properly between the buyer and the seller to avoid possible misunderstanding with regards to the responsibility of both parties. Theoretically speaking, the exporter insures the goods up to the point where the goods pass over the ship's rail and the buyer takes responsibility from then on in a FOB contract. However, in practice, the customer usually buys insurance to cover the whole journey in FOB contracts from the exporter's warehouse to the final destination.

(4)

The Contract is in octuplicate, four in the Chinese language and four in the English language. Each party shall keep 2 copies of both the English and the Chinese versions. Each copy of the Contract in either language shall have the same legal binding force. In the event of referring to arbitration when any dispute or conflict arises, a Chinese copy of the Contract and an English copy shall be submitted together. In the event of any dispute in the construe of the text of the Contract, the Chinese version shall prevail.

Exercises for Students(练习题)

(1)

Dear Kevin,

First of all, congratulations on meeting and exceeding our goals for school instrument sales in October! You worked on arranging for a trade-in for a completely new set of instruments and helped make October a month to remember.

I hope you will put the bonus check to good use, and continue to bring new ideas to the sales department.

Sincerely yours,

John Diamond

(2)

Vision and Mission

At CNOOC, we are guided by a path to sustainability (scientific outlook on development) and stay committed to win-win development, accountability, integrity, innovation and caring practices in everything we do. We work to achieve balanced growth and seek to grow and thrive by building the pipeline of future talent. We strive to stay ahead as a technological innovator and cost-effective producer. We identify and pursue distinctive growth opportunities in ways that help build a world-class energy producer with safe, efficient and strong operations.

(3)

Dear Mr. Jackman,

I am writing to inquire if your company has any opening in the area of food engineering. I have long been interested in working in your company.

Although I am a recent graduate with some intern experience, I still want to pursue a job which I find fascinating.

If any, please reply and I will send you a resume via Email. Thank you for your time.

Looking forward to hearing from you soon!

Yours sincerely,

Andy Carter

(4)

Give a Timex to all, and to all a good time.（Timex）

Good time, great taste, McDonald's .（McDonald）

If it wasn't in VOGUE, it wasn't in vogue.（VOGUE Fashion）

8.4 Translation on Business and Trade Discourses in English（商贸英语语篇的翻译）

商贸英语是在不同的商务场景中运用的英语，具有商务特色。外贸活动是一个国家的主要活动之一，英语是我国涉外经济活动中的主要交际语言。商贸英语有其自身的语言表达规律和特点，不了解这些规律和特点，就很难做好商贸汉英翻译工作。

1）用词简洁

从下面的这些商贸词语中，可以看出商贸英语用词的简洁。如：one price / fixed price 恕不讲价，year end sale 年终大甩卖，door-to-door service 一条龙服务，all sales are final 货物出门，概不退换，40% discount 6折优惠，freight forward 运费到付，in your favor 以你方为受益人等。从上述例子可以看出，商贸英语往往用一个名词短语表示一个句子的意思，言简意赅。

2）行业术语多

商贸英语在词汇使用上包含大量专业词汇，包括具有商务含义的普通词或复合词，以及缩略词等。翻译中最好选用商贸英语的专业术语，以求信息传递的准确性和有效性，例如：force majeure（不可抗拒力）、segmentation（市场细分）、counter-offer（还盘）、balance sheet（资产负债表）等。

3）缩略语多

使用缩略语能避免使用长而繁的表述，适应现代商务的需求。由于缩略词形式简练，带有行业特征的商贸英语缩略词便大量出现。例如：R&D（研发）、CWO（订货付现）、BL（提货单）等。

4）行文严谨

商贸英语所用词语要保证其国际通用性，其语体应介于正式体（formal）和商量体（consultative）之间。因此，过于简单化、口语化的某些介词和连词 because、about、if、like、for 等在商务英语中会被比较正式规范的介词短语所代替，比如：on the grounds that, with reference to，in the event/case of，in the nature of，for the purpose of 等。口语中常常使用的动词短语 go on，add to 被较为正式的单个动词 continue、supplement 所代替。

5）措辞委婉礼貌

商贸英语中的这种措辞婉转的表达方式折射出国际商贸领域既严格又灵活的语言规律。而汉英商贸语言的这种文体差异主要表现在句子的结构和用词上。例如，表达"你们的还价大大低于我方的成本，我们不能按你们的价格成交"。请看以下两种表达。

（1）I can not entertain business at your price, since it is far below our cost.

（2）I'm not in a position to entertain business at your price, since it is far below our cost.

以上两个句子基本都反映了所要表达的内容，但是仔细研究却发现语气不同。句（1）语气过于强硬，有失礼貌；句（2）则选用了"be not in a position to"这一结构，增添了客观所迫的感觉，语气缓和委婉。

鉴于商贸英语的种种特征，译者可采取以下翻译策略。

① 准确传达原文意思，把握专业词汇词义，根据上下文正确选择普通词汇词义。② 商贸英语凝练简洁的特征也同样要求译文的凝练简洁。为达到该目的，可以采用汉语四字结构或文言句式。例如："Thank you for your kind consideration."可译为"承蒙垂注，谨致谢意。""I venture to invite you to have a look at our stand, and you may rest assured that you will not be pressed to buy."可译为"本人冒昧地邀请贵方光顾我方展台，购买与否，悉听尊便。"③ 适当调整句子结构。商贸英语中经常出现长句、复合句、并列复合句等法律公文常用句式，以及分隔现象、介词（短语）、插入语、同位语、倒装句、被动语态、过去分词等句型。这时要用地道的、符合译入语风格的语言表达原文的意思。

Versions for Appreciation（译文赏析）

（1）The five Toyota, twenty Hitachi and thirty Xerox have long been ready for shipment, but shipment cannot be affected because of the late arrival of your L/C.

【译文】 5辆丰田牌汽车、20台日立牌空调和30台施乐牌复印机早已备妥待运，但因你方信用证延迟到达，货物不能按期装运。

【评析】 英语力求简洁，但在翻译成汉语时，需要从句法角度或逻辑关系角度，增补解释性的词汇，如动词、名词等，以使句意完整，译文通顺自然，符合汉语习惯。原文中的"Toyota""Hitachi""Xerox"都为世界知名品牌，在翻译时要按照汉语的习惯用法把他们的产品名称补充完整，才能使句意具体明了。在这里，译者增加了"汽车""空调""复印机"三种具体的商品名称，使句意更加准确完整。同时在商务英语中常会使用一些缩略词，如句中的"L/C"，指的是"信用证"，这要求译者多加积累，保证译文的准确性。

（2）The Employer hereby covenants to pay the Contractor in consideration of the execution and completion of the Works and the remedying of defects therein the Contract Price or such other sum as may become payable under the provisions of the Contract at the time and in the manner prescribed by the Contract.

【译文】 业主特此立约保证在合同规定的期限内，按合同规定的方式向承包人支付合同价，或合同规定的其他应支付的款项，以作为本工程施工、竣工及修补工程中缺陷的报酬。

【评析】 商务合同是合同双方签订并必须遵守的法律文件，因此合同中的语言应体现其权威性。英文合同用语的特点之一就表现在用词上，要使合同表达的意思准确无误，达到双方对合同中使用的词无可争议的程度。"hereby"通常为"by means of, by reason of this"的意思，常被译作"特此，因此，兹"等，常用于法律文件、合同、协议书等正式文件的开头语，在条款中需要强调时也可使用，传达一种正式庄重，严肃谨慎之感。

（3）Principal hereby appoints agent as its exclusive agent to sell products in Territory, within and to the extent of the right granted hereunder, on behalf of Principal and Agent accepts and assumes such appointment.

【译文】 委托人兹委托代理人为其独家代理，代表委托人，在本条款所给予的权利限度内，在所定"地区"销售指定"产品"，代理人接受并承担该项委托。

【评析】 该句中，有"accepts and assumes"和"within and to the extent of"两个成对的同义词或相关的词。这种情况在商贸英语中很常见，这些词语体现了商贸英语行文严谨、表述正规的特点，在翻译时不能机械对等，否则译文会拖沓冗长。这里"accepts and assumes"可译为"接受并承担"以加强口气，"within and to the extent of"可视为一个整体，译为"在……限度之内"。另外，原句中有普通名词首字母大写的情况，这在商贸英语中往往有指定之意，但在汉语中没有办法区别大小写字母，译文通过增加"所定"二字和引号表达。原文采用了多个介词结构做状语，在翻译时译者采用了直译，将其一一对应译出，保证了译文对原文的忠实。

（4）The furniture we ordered from you should have reached us a week ago. The delay in delivery has put us to great inconvenience. It is therefore imperative that you dispatch them immediately. Otherwise, we shall be obliged to cancel the order and obtain the goods elsewhere.

【译文】 我方从贵方订购的家具应于一星期前收到。发货的延迟给我方带来了很大的不便。因此，贵方必须立即发货，否则我们将被迫取消订单，到别处订货。

【评析】 原文为一封抱怨和索赔信函，此类信函的目的是获取更好的服务，对已出现的问题求得快速的、妥善的解决。因此在翻译时应当开门见山，提出条件，表达不满，并提出解决方案。译文仅用两句话指明问题所在，并提出影响，内容清楚、有理、明确，将"imperative"译作"必须立即"，语气坚决，传达坚定的态度。同时，为了避免使用愤怒和使对方难堪的措辞，译者使用"我方"和"贵方"来表达委婉的语气。

（5）Party A shall have a right of first refusal whenever party B wishes to sell any of its shares in the Group.

【译文】 乙方任何时候有意出售其持有之本集团任何股份，甲方一律拥有优先购买权。

【评析】 在不涉及特殊文化背景因素的情况下，译者可以选择转换表达角度，用目标语意义替代源语意义，重组源语信息的表层形式，以使译文更加符合汉语习惯，更易于被读者接受，有利于实现译文预期功能。在此句中，如果把"right of first refusal"翻译成"优先拒绝权"，则不够准确，译者需要通过视角转换将其译成"优先购买权"才符合行业规范。

商贸英语包括多种文体，其中应用文体最为常见，这里我们简要介绍商务信函和电文的文体特点和翻译。

Questions for Teacher's Lecture（讲解题）

Translate the following passages into Chinese.

（1）

In the event that the proceeding of the cooperative program ceases or either party quits the program with reasons, a party shall and shall urge its representatives to destroy or return to the other party all confidential information as well as all documents and materials and all duplicates thereof containing confidential information within five working days, upon the request of the other party at any time. Nevertheless, the party possessing the confidential information may keep one piece of the duplicates of the documents or materials described above only for the purpose enshrined in Article 4 hereunder, without breaching other provisions of this agreement.

Disclosure of the confidential information by either Party A or Party B to the other party or its representatives shall not be construed to constitute an assignment or grant to the other party or its representatives of the rights and interests in relation to its trade secrets, trademarks, patents, know-how or any other intellectual property, nor shal l it constitute an assignment or grant to the other party or its representatives the rights and interests in relation to the trade secrets, trademarks, patents, know-how, or any other intellectual property authorized by a third party.

（2）

Dear Sirs,

Thank you for your letter of 25th September.

As one of the largest dealers of garments, we are interested in dresses of all descriptions. We would be grateful if you would give us quotations per dozen of C.L.F. Vancouver for those items as listed on the separate sheet. In the meantime, we would like you to send us samples of the various materials of which the dresses are made.

We are given to understand that you are a state-owned enterprise and we have confidence in the quality of Chinese products. If your prices are moderate, we believe there is a promising market for the above-mentioned articles area.

We look forward to hearing from you soon.

Your faithfully,

Canadian Garment Co.

Exercises for Students（练习题）

Translate the following passage into Chinese.

To be packed in strong wooden cases or cartons, suitable for long distance ocean, parcel post or air freight transportation as well as changing climate and with good resistance to moisture and shocks.

The Seller shall be liable for any damage of the commodity due to improper packing and for any rust attributable to inadequate protective measures in regard to the packing.

One full set of service and operation manual shall be enclosed in each case.

参考文献

[1] 王佐良. 英国诗史[M]. 南京：江苏译林出版社，2008.

[2] 许渊冲. 文学与翻译[M]. 北京：北京大学出版社，2003.

[3] 许渊冲. 翻译的艺术[M]. 北京：五洲传播出版社，2006.

[4] 李公昭. 新编英国文学选读[M]. 西安：西安交通大学出版社，2000.

[5] 傅雷. 翻译论集[M]. 北京：商务印书馆，1984.

[6] 冯庆华. 实用翻译教程[M]. 上海：上海外语教育出版社，2019.

[7] 杨士焯. 英汉翻译教程[M]. 北京：北京大学出版社，2006.

[8] 李运兴. 英汉语篇翻译[M]. 北京：清华大学出版社，2003.

[9] 连淑能. 英译汉教程[M]. 北京：高等教育出版社，2006.

[10] 陈生保. 英汉翻译津指[M]. 北京：中国对外翻译出版公司，1998.

[11] 杨全红. 高级翻译十二讲[M]. 武汉：武汉大学出版社，2009.

[12] 方梦之. 实用文本汉译英[M]. 青岛：青岛出版社，2003.

[13] 王恩冕. 大学英汉翻译教程[M]. 北京：对外经济贸易大学出版社，2004.

[14] 蔡基刚. 英汉汉英段落翻译与实践[M]. 上海：复旦大学出版社，2001.

[15] 孙致礼. 翻译理论与实践探索》[M]. 南京：译林出版社，1999.

[16] 范仲英. 实用翻译教程》[M]. 北京：外语教育与研究出版社，1994.

[17] 胡卫平. 大学英语翻译[M]. 上海：同济大学出版社，2001.

[18] 仲伟合. 英语口译教程：下[M]. 北京：高等教育出版社，2006.